Aaron Copland

Aaron Copland
A Guide to Research

Marta Robertson
and Robin Armstrong

Composer Resource Manual
Number 53

Routledge
New York and London

Published in 2001 by
Routledge
29 West 35th Street
New York, NY 10001

Published in in Great Britain by
Routledge
11 New Fetter Lane
London EC4P 4EE

Routledge is an imprint of the Taylor & Francis Group

10 9 8 7 6 5 4 3 2 1

Library of Congress Cataloging-in-Publication Data
Robertson, Marta.
    Aaron Copland : a guide to reserach / Marta Robertson and
Robin Armstrong.
        p. cm. — (Composer resource manuals ; v. 53) (Garland
    reference library of the humanities ; vol. 1957)
    Includes bibliographical references and indexes.
    Discography: p.
    ISBN 0-8153-2178-3 (alk. paper)
    1. Copland, Aaron, 1900–1990—Bibliography.   I. Armstrong,
    Robin, 1959-   II. Title.   III. Series.   IV. Routledge composer
    resource
manuals ; v. 53.

    ML134.C66 R63 2000
    016.78'092—dc21   99-089420

Printed on acid-free, 250-year-life paper
Manufactured in the United States of America

Composer Resource Manuals

In response to the growing need for bibliographic guidance to the vast literature on significant composers, Routledge is publishing an extensive series of research guides. This ongoing series encompasses more than 50 composers; they represent Western musical tradition from the Renaissance to the present century.

Each research guide offers a selective, annotated list of writings, in all European languages, about one or more composers. There are also lists of works by the composers, unless these are available elsewhere. Biographical sketches and guides to library resources, organizations, and specialists are presented. As appropriate to the individual composer, there are maps, photographs or other illustrative matter, glossaries, and indexes.

Contents

Preface

Aaron Copland is generally considered the most popular and best known composer of American art music. Although many Americans are familiar with his music—whether from concerts, television commercials, or film spin-offs—scholarly evaluation of Copland and his works waned after the 1950s. Until the mid-1980s, most overviews of Copland's oeuvre were found either in music history texts, among the obligatory three pages per composer, or in the two classic monographs completed in the 1950s, prior to the conclusion of Copland's career.[1] Copland's exhaustive two-volume autobiography, coauthored with Vivian Perlis,[2] Howard Pollack's definitive biography,[3] and recent dissertations and theses by a new generation of scholars suggest a current resurgence of interest in Copland.

Ironically, while Copland's compositions traditionally have received relatively little attention in the specialist literature, the opposite problem—that of perhaps too much exposure—exists when tributes to Copland, announcements of his activities, or reviews of his compositions are concerned. Practically every musical journal announced his momentous birthdays every five years, while most ensembles from high schools to professional orchestras have at some time programmed his compositions. The primary purpose of *Aaron Copland: A Guide to Research* is to direct readers to significant sources for information on Copland's life, compositions, musical activities, and cultural context.

In *Aaron Copland: A Guide to Research*, the chapter organization reflects an ordering of bibliographic importance, moving from general information on Copland to primary and then secondary

sources. Section II, "Chronology of Life and Works," is a chronological chart simultaneously representing three concurrent spheres
of Copland's career: biography, compositions, and writings. The
chart makes tangible the methodological conviction that Copland's
life can best be studied in the context of his compositions and writings, and vice versa. It is assumed that the reader will consult the
article on Copland by William Austin in the *New Grove Dictionary
of American Music*,[4] or similar works cited in Section IV, for prose
biographies. In addition, the reader should consult the *New Grove
Dictionary of American Music*, Joann Skowronski's *Aaron Copland: A Bio-Bibliography*,[5] or Pollack's *Aaron Copland: The Life
and Work of an Uncommon Man* for a work-list containing information on manuscripts and premieres. The chronological compilation of Copland's writings in Section II should be cross-referenced
with the alphabetical annotations in Section III. Section I, "A Guide
to Studies on Aaron Copland," is a survey of trends in research,
with suggestions for additional avenues of exploration.

Section III, "Primary Sources—Copland's Writings," is a comprehensive list, with annotations, of Copland's published and
unpublished books, articles, essays, and interviews.[6] The principal
resources for Section III were the *Guide to the Aaron Copland Collection at the Library of Congress* (available in the Music Division
of the Library of Congress), *The Music Index, Aaron Copland: A
Bio-Bibliography*, and bibliographies in secondary sources. At the
time that Skowronski's *Aaron Copland: A Bio-Bibliography* was
written, before Copland's death, many of his manuscripts had not
been transferred to the Library of Congress. Because Copland's
writings often were published outside of the traditional musical literature, the comprehensive listings of this section were previously
impossible without full access to his manuscripts and the proliferation of electronic databases. Section III also includes unpublished
manuscripts of articles and essays, held in the Copland Collection,
chronicling the full extent of Copland's literary activities.[7] It is
hoped that future scholars may locate publication data for those
manuscripts currently cataloged as unpublished or undated.

The selection criteria for citations in the chapters of secondary sources are necessarily different than those for the comprehensive primary source chapter. Skowronski's *Aaron Copland:
A Bio-Bibliography* is commendably thorough through 1984.
Since *Aaron Copland: A Guide to Research* is meant to comple-
ment, rather than duplicate, Skowronski's effort, the majority of

the citations refer to significant secondary sources written since 1983—writings encompassing the end of Copland's career, his death in 1990, and the concurrent revival of scholarly interest leading up to the centenary of his birth in 2000.[8] The citations since 1983 were culled from *The Music Index, RILM Abstracts, Dissertation Abstracts International,* and *Humanities Index.* The secondary source material prior to 1983 is extremely selective—works either primarily or exclusively about Copland—and is culled mainly from *RILM Abstracts.* The reader should consult Skowronski's bibliography for additional sources prior to 1983. Secondary sources are limited primarily to books, articles, and dissertations or theses in English; for newspaper references such as society news and book, performance, or record reviews, readers should consult Skowronski's bibliography and newspaper indices such as *The New York Times Index.*[9]

Section IV, "Secondary Sources—General Studies on Copland's Life and Milieu," is arranged by bibliographic importance from comprehensive studies, to significant references in monographs, to major articles in journals, encyclopedias, Web sites, and videotapes. Section V, "Secondary Sources—Writings about Copland's Compositions," is organized from larger compositional issues to examinations of specific genres or works. Section VI, "Topical Studies," reflects Copland's multidisciplinary contributions within the superstructure of American musical culture, an issue about which he wrote passionately. We hope that by organizing Section VI topically, we prompt future scholars to begin thorough explorations of the full range of Copland's contributions as conductor, critic, commentator, author, mentor, and teacher, in addition to composer and musician.

Section VII is a listing of tributes and obituaries, which are not annotated because of the repetitive content of the sources. Although *Aaron Copland: A Guide to Research* was not initially limited to English-language secondary sources, the presence of only one reference in Section VIII confirms that the significant research on Copland, readily available in North American libraries through interlibrary loan, is almost exclusively published in English. Because of the meteoric rate of change in the recording industry, Copland's recordings are not annotated; instead, historical discographies and Internet locations functioning as current discographies are included with traditional bibliographies in Section IX. An extensive subject index is included with the traditional author and title indexes. As a result, future scholars can analyze topical writings by Copland in conjunction with his concurrent compositions and related secondary source research—whether on the development of South American music, the institution of musical criticism in the United States, or the promotion of an identifiably American music.

Finally, we both would like to acknowledge the financial assistance of Gettysburg College and Western Maryland College in support of *Aaron Copland: A Guide to Research*. In addition, we would like to thank our students, especially Karen Cook, who have helped in the research process.

Notes

1. Arthur Berger, *Aaron Copland* (New York: Oxford University, 1953), and Julia F. Smith, *Aaron Copland: His Work and Contribution to American Music* (New York: E. P. Dutton, 1955).
2. Aaron Copland and Vivian Perlis, *Copland: 1900 through 1942* (New York: St. Martin's/Marek, 1984), and Aaron Copland and Vivian Perlis, *Copland: Since 1942* (New York: St. Martin's, 1989).
3. Howard Pollack, *Aaron Copland: The Life and Work of an Uncommon Man* (New York: Henry Holt, 1999).
4. William H. Austin, "Copland," vol. 1, *The New Grove Dictionary of American Music*, ed. H. Wiley Hitchcock and Stanley Sadie (London: Macmillan, 1986).
5. Joann Skowronski, *Aaron Copland: A Bio-Bibliography* (Westport, CT: Greenwood, 1985).
6. Throughout *Aaron Copland: A Guide to Research*, annotations are based on examination of the items, unless stated otherwise. Each bibliographic entry contains pagination information, an International Standard Book Number (ISBN), and Library of Congress (LC) call number, when appropriate.
7. Copland's unpublished lectures, speeches, and correspondence are not included in Section III, because they are currently available only at the Library of Congress. While this is also true of Copland's unpublished articles or essays, we include them to illustrate the comprehensive scope of his published writings; many of these unpublished manuscripts became drafts for later publications.
8. The Interviews category in Section III is similarly selective.
9. Such secondary source material is occasionally annotated in *Aaron Copland: A Guide to Research*, as are selected tributes or obituaries, if the article includes significant historical information.

AARON COPLAND

I. A Guide to Studies on Aaron Copland

> The house inside is comfortable, clean-lined,
> uncluttered. The living–dining room has paintings
> on the walls, abstract and realistic. "They don't
> go together," said Aaron. "But they're all painted
> by my friends." . . . The studio is dominated by
> the piano and a large table-desk the composer has
> had for thirty years. It was made for him by an-
> other friend and has a double top; in the space
> between he files letters and work sheets.[1]

If a living and working space could be a metaphor for someone's professional career, then Aaron Copland's home paralleled his life-long musical concerns. In his workspace, his piano, desk, scores, letters, books, manuscripts, recordings, and a set of the Grove *Dictionary of Music and Musicians* all coexisted. Throughout his personal and professional life Copland similarly was surrounded by a context of friends, students, colleagues, critics, teachers, listeners, readers, lovers, family, commentators, and musicians. He composed at the piano, but the desk from which he conducted other musical activities simultaneously encapsulated a profession and a friendship.

Copland's compositions—sometimes atonal, other times diatonic, but all communicative and sensitive to the musical purpose and materials of the composition—are analogous to the pictures on his walls. While a casual visitor perceived tension between the realistic and abstract paintings, the works were united in the context of gifts from friends. In much the same way, many commentators have categorized Copland's compositions as either programmatic or abstract, failing to recognize the Americanism and individual compositional style—an aesthetic that, like his home, was "clean-lined, uncluttered"[2]—that unified Copland's works.

So often academic research decontextualizes its subject in favor of structural analyses that prove the importance of the object being analyzed, thus simultaneously elevating the researcher in the process. Few composers will benefit more than Copland from the current move of scholarly research toward increasing contextualization and inclusivity. Copland, even when composing his most erudite works, was no ivory-tower composer. His lifelong concerns of musical communication, promotion of the living composer, and establishment of an identifiably American musical expression placed him in the center of musical activity in the United States throughout much of the twentieth century.

During his lifetime, Copland chafed against his typecasting as solely a composer of Americana, with its implications of frontier narratives, quotations of folk music, and accessibility to the general listener. Similarly, he challenged the dichotomization of his works as either "serious" or "popular." Although quipping, "I have a split personality,"[3] Copland concluded the emendation of "Composer from Brooklyn: An Autobiographical Sketch" by stating:

> I can only say that those commentators who would like to split me down the middle into two opposing personalities will get no encouragement from me. I prefer to think that I write my music from a single vision; when the results differ it is because I take into account with each new piece the purpose for which it is intended and the nature of the musical materials with which I begin to work. . . . It bothers me not at all to realize that my range as composer includes both accessible and problematic works.[4]

Despite such statements, scholars and critics frequently have reinforced the polarization of Copland's compositions, superimposing musical dichotomies—popular/serious, programmatic/abstract, tonal/atonal, and diatonic/serial—on divisive chronological periods.[5] It seems neither profitable nor appropriate to continue to study Copland in relative isolation or through outdated categorizations, especially when the documentary record left by Copland suggests otherwise.

Recent research on Copland has begun to emphasize the unities among his works, whether through compositional style or Americanism. As Larry Starr has argued, it is precisely the heterogeneity of Copland's compositions, reflecting the diversity and plurality of American culture, that unifies and defines his musical Americanism.[6] Underlying the heterogeneity and supposed dichotomies, Starr identified a pervasive Coplandesque style based on "melodic variation—where a basic cell is gradually expanded into a longer unit (without departing too far from the content of the basic cell itself) through a process of repetition, reordering, and the accretion or interpolation of new elements."[7] A profitable direction for future research is to apply the compositional principles identified by Copland and Starr not just to individual pieces, but to chronological periods consisting of diverse genres, or specific genres crossing apparent compositional or chronological styles.

Given Copland's notoriety as a composer, his relative scholarly neglect indicates previous academic biases against much of his music. As Starr stated, the "specifically American qualities" of Copland's music have led "*American* critics, academics, and intelligentsia" to undervalue his compositions.[8] The scholarly underevaluation of Copland is intensified in his collaborative works because of their "functional" associations and in his "Americana" scores because of their popular appeal. The scholarly bias toward decontextualized theoretical analyses of Copland's abstract works is also clear. The challenge of future Copland studies is to bridge the gap between the now-dated dichotomies—to contextualize (even humanize) the theoretical analyses applied to abstract compositions, and to develop critical methodologies that substantiate the collaborative and multidisciplinary compositions. With all of Copland's manuscripts and letters now available at the Library of Congress, in addition to his published compositions and unpublished musical manuscripts, it is possible to evaluate Copland's musical contributions in the context of his other professional and personal activities.

Aaron Copland: A Guide to Research has been designed to assess the areas of Copland's compositional and professional career that have been neglected in scholarly study. In Section II, the chronological chart of Copland's biography, compositions, and writings is intended to encourage the contextualization of all three areas for future Copland studies. The comprehensive collection and annotation of Copland's published writings and unpublished manuscripts (Section III) allows not only access to the content of these writings but also the potential for future research to address the scope of his literary efforts.

A perusal of the secondary sources (Sections IV–VI) suggests methodological avenues for continued exploration. For example, in Section IV.A, Howard Pollack's definitive biography serves as a model for contextualization of Copland's career within the spheres of his sexuality, his artistic circles (especially dance), and his literary influences.[9] The works by Copland and Vivian Perlis provide the commentary by Copland to support these expanded directions. In Section IV.B, Jennifer DeLapp's dissertation suggests a profitable methodological model for balancing contextual and theoretical analyses of specific compositions. Previously, articles by Carol Oja and Robert Parker have provided similar methodological directions.

Before a full syntheses of Copland's compositional style or evaluations of complete genres can be undertaken, individual studies of specific compositions must create the foundation. Section V is structured to indicate the compositional techniques, genres, and individual works that have been most overlooked. Section V.B.1. shows that this type of research on the individual ballets has occurred. Because of the interdisciplinary nature of dance, these studies tend to be relatively contextualized. While the film scores and incidental music should present a similar opportunity, studies of these genres lag behind since many of the scores remain unpublished in their entirety and because these compositions have not achieved repertory status as suites, divorced from their collaborative context. Methodologies that unite the musical elements with the visual, narrative, and psychological components of the film, choreography, or text need to be explored further.

Many of the studies of specific instrumental compositions reflect the graduate degree requirements of academic institutions. Instrumental performers tend to study the repertoire of their specific instrument; thus, the solo repertory—the Clarinet Concerto, the *Duo* for flute and piano, and especially the solo piano works—has received concentrated attention. Singers, choral directors, and instrumental conductors have not similarly mined Copland's oeuvre. For example, no significant work has been focused specifically on

Copland's orchestration, one of the most telling aspects of his unique compositional style. While his two operas and especially the *Twelve Poems of Emily Dickinson* have been studied, the remainder of Copland's vocal works await substantial examination.

With recent efforts to contextualize Copland within a broadened definition of musical Americanism, Section VI.A should become more substantial. Additionally, the corpus of Copland's writings as critic, commentator, and/or author needs to be examined systematically, especially in conjunction with concurrent compositions or musical activities.[10] Given that the final three decades of Copland's professional life (1956–1983) centered on his conducting, rather than composing, it is a major oversight that this area of his musical activities has not been studied. Through his conducting, Copland's musical philosophies literally were taken from the written and musical page and put into motion. For example, the programming of concerts that Copland conducted reflects his life-long commitment to the promotion of contemporary music, particularly that of the living American composer.

Similarly, as "Dean of American Composers, " Copland's role of mentor and teacher to young composers from as early as 1926 through the mid-1960s has not been explored thoroughly. Just as Robert Schumann promoted the compositional career of Johannes Brahms, Copland did for four generations of young American composers. Each decade Copland routinely assessed the younger generation of composers, listing almost exclusively men. Was it his amazing perceptivity or a self-fulfilling prophecy that such a high percentage of these composers rose to national prominence—and women continued to compose in relative obscurity—through the 1960s?

As we begin the new century of research on Copland, it is no longer necessary to carry forward outdated assumptions—whether methodological models, obstinate categorizations of "serious" and "popular" music, or other academic biases. As each of the specific areas to which Copland contributed is better understood, a full synthesis of his career can be realized.

Let the latest research begin!

Notes

1. Dorle J. Soria, "Artist's Life," *High Fidelity/Musical America* 20 (November 1970): MA-4. Soria described Aaron Copland's home near Peekskill, New York, during an interview conducted in 1970.

2. Ibid.

3. Aaron Copland, "Composer from Brooklyn: An Autobiographical Sketch," in *The New Music, 1900–1960* (New York: W. W. Norton, 1968), 163.

4. Ibid., 168.

5. The traditional categorizations of Copland's compositions have been called into question by authors such as Lawrence Starr, who has proposed elements of a unified compositional style (Lawrence Starr, "Copland's Style," *Perspectives of New Music* 19 [Fall–Winter 980]: 87–88).

6. Larry Starr, "Ives, Gershwin, and Copland: Reflections on the Strange History of American Art Music," *American Music* 12 (Summer 1994): 168–169. In this case, "Americanism" implies the larger American musical palette referred to by Copland and Starr, while "Americana" implies the specific expression of Americanism associated with the frontier, musical accessibility, and the quotation of folk tunes.

7. Ibid., 181.

8. Ibid., 179.

9. Howard Pollack, *Aaron Copland: The Life and Work of an Uncommon Man* (New York: Henry Holt, 1999). Pollack's book initiated the wave of research surrounding the centenary of Copland's birth in 2000.

10. Pollack's biography does cover each of these areas, but there is considerable room for systematic application of these musical endeavors to individual compositions by Copland.

II. Chronology of Life and Works

The chronological outline presented in this section was compiled primarily from Joann Skowronski, *Aaron Copland: A Bio-Bibliography* (Westport, CT: Greenwood, 1985); William W. Austin, "Copland," *New Grove Dictionary of American Music*, ed. by H. Wiley Hitchcock and Stanley Sadie, vol. 1 (London: Macmillan, 1986), 496–504; Howard Pollack, *Aaron Copland: The Life and Work of an Uncommon Man* (New York: Henry Holt, 1999); Copland, *The New Music, 1900–1960* (New York: W. W. Norton, 1968); and the *Guide to the Aaron Copland Collection at the Library of Congress* (available in the Music Division of the Library of Congress). For prose accounts of Copland's life and works, refer to Sections IV.A, IV.C, and IV.D. The citations in this first column are arranged chronologically by year, but not necessarily chronologically within each year.

Copland's writings—both published and unpublished—and interviews are arranged chronologically by year and alphabetically within a year. Interviews are identified by an (I) following the title. The outline is meant to provide a chronological listing of the primary sources arranged alphabetically and annotated in Section III. Articles and manuscripts without a known date are listed alphabetically following the chart.

The shortened chart format is meant as an abbreviated reference to the compositions. To portray the full scope of Copland's compositional activities by year, we include unpublished works, arrangements, and revisions under the year of activity, rather than under the year of composition of the original work. Compositions are arranged chronologically by year, beginning with the start date of their composition, and are arranged by genre within each year. The genre appears within brackets, with the following categories: opera, ballet, film scores [film], incidental music [incd], orchestral [orch], symphonic band [sym band], brass ensemble [brass], chamber [cham], keyboard [kb], choral [chor], and songs [song]. Compositions without a known date are listed alphabetically after the chart. The chronological work-list was compiled primarily from Joann Skowronski, *Aaron Copland: A Bio-Bibliography*, William W. Austin, "Copland," and Howard Pollack, *Aaron Copland: The Life and Work of an Uncommon Man*. For complete premiere information, refer to Pollack and Skowronski. For work-lists by genre, refer to Pollack and Austin. For alphabetical listings, see Boosey & Hawkes's Web site.

Year	Biography	Writings	Compositions
1900	November 14: Born in Brooklyn, New York		
1908~	Age 7: Began piano lessons with sister, Laurine		
1909~	Age 8: Wrote first composition for sister-in-law		
1913	1913–17: Formal piano lessons with Leopold Wolfsohn		
1916			*Capriccio* [cham]
1917	1917–19: Piano studies with Victor Wittgenstein Fall: Began studies with Rubin Gold-mark, continued for four years		*Moment Musicale* [kb] "Melancholy" [song] "Spurned Love" [song] "After Antwerp" [song]
1918	Spring: Graduated from Boys' High School in Brooklyn		*Poème* [cham] *Waltz Caprice* [kb] *Sonnet I* [kb] *Three Songs*: "My Heart Is in the East," "A Summer Vacation," "Night" [song]
1919	1919–21: Piano studies with Clarence Adler		*Lament* [cham] *Lament*, arr. pf trio, incomplete [cham] Preludes I and II (1919, 1921) [cham] *Sonnet II* [kb] "Simone" [song]

Year	Biography	Writings	Compositions
1920			*Sonnet III* [kb]
			Humoristic Scherzo: The Cat and the Mouse [kb]
			Three Moods: "Embittered," "Wistful," "Jazzy" (1920–21) [kb]
			"Music I Heard" [song]
			"Old Poem" [song]
1921	June: Composition studies at Fontainebleau School of Music with Paul Vidal		*Sonata Movement on a Theme by Paul Vidal* [cham]
	December: Honorable mention, Prix de Paris		Piano Sonata [kb]
			Petit Portrait [kb]
			Passacaglia (1921–22) [kb]
	1921-Fall 1924: Studied with Nadia Boulanger in Paris		*Four Motets* [chor]
			"Pastorale" [song]
			"Une Chanson" [song]
			"Reconnaissance" [song]
1922			*Grohg* (1922–25) [ballet]
			"Alone" [song]
1923			*Cortège Macabre* (from *Grohg*) [orch]
			Movement, c. 1923 [cham]
			Two Pieces: "Rondino" (1923) "Lento Molto" (1928) [cham]
			"As It Fell upon a Day" [song]

Year	Biography	Writings	Compositions
1924	Boulanger requested organ solo piece for New York Symphony performance and her first American tour June: Returned to United States, tried to establish himself as private teacher Fall: League of Composers sponsored concert with *The Cat and the Mouse* and Passacaglia. First works performed in U.S. October: Established first Manhattan residence	"Gabriel Fauré, a Neglected Master"	*Organ Symphony* [orch] "Jazz Song" (c. 1924) [song]
1925	1925, 1926: First composer to be awarded a Guggenheim, renewed following year January 11: Walter Damrosch premiered Symphony for Organ and Orchestra with the New York Symphony, Boulanger as soloist Summer: MacDowell Colony, working on League of Composers commission, instigated by Koussevitzky	"George Antheil" "[Letter to the Editor] Defends the Music of Mahler" "What Europe Means to the Aspiring Composer"	*Music for the Theatre* (Suite in Five Parts) [orch] "The House on the Hill" [chor] "An Immorality" [chor]

Year	Biography	Writings	Compositions
1926	Israel Citkowitz, Copland's first protégé Summer: Returned to Europe	"America's Young Men of Promise" "Playing Safe at Zurich"	*Organ Symphony* arr. w/o org as Symphony no. 1, (1926–28) [from orch] Piano Concerto [orch] *Two Pieces*: "Nocturne," "Ukelele Serenade" [cham] "Blues No. 1" (pub. as *Sentimental Melody: Slow Dance*) [kb] "Blues No. 2" (pub. as *Four Piano Blues*, no. 4) [kb]
1927	Summer: Returned to Europe 1927–37: Lecturer in Music, New School for Social Research, New York, led to *What to Listen for in Music* and *Our New Music*	"Forecast and Review: Baden-Baden, 1927" "Jazz Structure and Influence"	*Symphonic Ode* (1927–29) [orch] "Poet's Song" [song]
1928	Joined League of Composers 1928–31: Organized Copland-Sessions Concerts with Roger Sessions	"Carlos Chávez—Mexican Composer" "Music Since 1920" "Stravinsky's *Oedipus Rex*"	"Prelude" (from *Organ Sym.*) arr. chamber orch [from orch] *Two Pieces*: "Rondino" (1923) "Lento Molto" (1928) arr. str orch [from cham] *Vitebsk (Study on a Jewish Theme)* [cham] "Vocalise" [song]

Year	Biography	Writings	Compositions
1929	Founded Cos Cob Press, later Arrow Music Press	"From a Composer's Notebook"	*Dance Symphony* (from *Grohg*) [orch]
	Introduced to Paul Bowles by Henry Cowell	"The Lyricism of Milhaud"	
	Summer: Returned to Europe		
	Completion of *Symphonic Ode*, written for 50th anniversary of Boston Symphony Orchestra		
	RCA Victor Award of $25,000 offered; Copland eventually won $5,000		
1930		"Modern Orchestration Surveyed"	*Piano Variations* [kb]
		"A Note on Nadia Boulanger"	
1931	Summer: In Tangier with Paul Bowles, at suggestion of Gertrude Stein	"Contemporaries at Oxford: 1931"	*Miracle at Verdun*, chamber orch [incd]
1932	Founded American Festivals of Contemporary Music, Yaddo, Saratoga Springs, New York (continued 1933)	"The Composer and His Critic"	*Grohg*, rev. [ballet]
		"Stravinsky and Hindemith Premieres"	*Short Symphony* (Symphony no. 2) (1932–33) [orch]
	Visited Mexico at invitation of Carlos Chávez		*El Salón México* (1932–36) [orch]
	Began serving on Board of Directors, League of Composers		*Elegies* [cham]

Year	Biography	Writings	Compositions
1933		"The Composer in America, 1923–1933"	"Dance of the Adolescent" (from *Grohg*), arr. 2 pf [from ballet]
1934	"Into the Streets May First" published	"One Hundred and Fourteen Songs"	*Hear Ye! Hear Ye!* [ballet]
		"Workers Sing!"	"Into the Streets May First" [chor]
1935	Spring: Taught composition at Harvard University	"The American Composer Gets a Break"	*Statements*: "Militant," "Cryptic," "Dogmatic," "Subjective," "Jingo," "Prophetic" [orch]
		"A Note on Young Composers"	*Sunday Afternoon Music* [kb]
		"Scherchen on Conducting and Ewen on Composers"	*The Young Pioneers* [kb]
			"What Do We Plant?" [chor]
1936	*El Salón México* led to a permanent contract with Boosey & Hawkes	"Active Market in New Music Records"	*The Second Hurricane* [opera]
		"Our Younger Generation Ten Years Later"	
		"Pioneer Listener"	
		"Scores and Records"	
1937	CBS commissioned *Music for Radio: Saga of the Prairie*	"Mexican Composer"	*Prairie Journal* (formerly *Music for Radio: Saga of the Prairie*) [orch]
	Met Leonard Bernstein on Copland's birthday	"Scores and Records"	*Sextet* (arr. of *Short Symphony*) [cham]
	1937–45: Cofounder and president of American Composers Alliance	"Scores and Records"	
		"Scores and Records."	
		"Scores and Records"	
		"The World of the Phonograph"	

Year	Biography	Writings	Compositions
1938	1938–72: Cofounder and treasurer of Arrow Music Press	"Notes on a Cowboy Ballet" "Scores and Records" "Scores and Records" "Scores and Records" "Scores and Records"	*Billy the Kid* [ballet] *Signature* [orch] *An Outdoor Overture* [orch] "Lark" [chor] "We've Come" ("Banu") [song]
1939	*From Sorcery to Science* produced for 1939 World's Fair	"Composer from Brooklyn" "The Creative Process in Music" "The Live Composer" "Melody" "New Records" "Scores and Records" "The Story Behind *El Salón México*" "Thomson's Musical State" *What to Listen for in Music*	*Billy the Kid*, orch suite [from ballet] *The City* [film] *Of Mice and Men* [film] *The Five Kings* [incd] *Quiet City* [incd] *From Sorcery to Science (Music for a Puppet Show)*, orch [incd] Piano Sonata (1939–41) [kb]
1940	Began 25-year association with Berkshire Music Center at Tanglewood as teacher, adviser, and later chair of the faculty	"The Aims of Music for Films" "The Composers Get Wise" "Is There a Revolution in the Arts?" "The Musical Scene Changes" "Second Thoughts on Hollywood" Strauss, Theodore. "What Music Has Charms?" (I)	*Our Town* [film] *Our Town*, orch suite [from film] "Story of Our Town" (from *Our Town*) arr. vn, pf [from film] *Quiet City* suite for tpt, Eng hrn, strings [from incd] *John Henry* [orch] *Episode* [kb]

Year	Biography	Writings	Compositions
1941	Brooklyn College temporary position	"Five Post-Romantics"	
	Toured 7 South American countries sponsored by sub-committee of the Federal Coordinator of Inter-American Relations	"Music in Cuba"	
		"La música en el extranjero"	
		Our New Music; Leading Composers in Europe and America	
		"Some Notes on my *Music for the Theatre*"	
1942	André Kostelanetz commissioned musical portraits of American heroes, leading to *Lincoln Portrait*	"The Composers of South America"	*Rodeo* [ballet]
		"Latin Americans in Music"	*4 dance episodes* (from *Rodeo*) orch [from ballet]
	August: Elizabeth Sprague Coolidge commissioned *Appalachian Spring*	"[Letter to Editor] From the Mail Pouch: The Composers Ob[ject]: A Response from Eleven Who Were Represented at Critics' Concerts"	*An Outdoor Overture*, arr. sym band [from orch]
			Lincoln Portrait [orch]
	Elected member in Department of Music, National Institute of Arts and Letters		*Music for Movies* (from film scores for *The City*, *Of Mice and Men*, *Our Town*) [orch]
			Fanfare for the Common Man [sym band]
			Sonata for Violin and Piano (1942–43) [cham]
			Danzón Cubano [kb]
			"Las Agachadas" ("The Shake-Down Song") [chor]
1943		"From the '20's to the '40's and Beyond"	*Appalachian Spring* (1943–44) [ballet]

Year	Biography	Writings	Compositions
		"Listening to Poly-phonic Music"	*The North Star* [film]
		"Marc Blitzstein"	"Song of the Guer-rillas" (from *The North Star*) nar, TTBB, pf [chor]
		"The Modern Symphony"	
			"Song of the Guer-rillas" (from *The North Star*) voice, pf [song]
1944	Fall: Taught at Harvard University	"On the Notation of Rhythm"	*Our Town*, 3 ex-cerpts arr. pf [from film]
		"Serge Kousse-vitzky and the American Com-poser"	*Letter from Home* [orch]
			Symphony no. 3 (1944–46) [orch]
			Midday Thoughts (1944/1982) [kb]
1945	Awarded Pulitzer Prize for *Appalachian Spring*	"The American Composer Today"	*Appalachian Spring* suite, orch [from ballet]
	Won New York Music Critics' Circle Award for *Appalachian Spring*	"American Music since 1930"	*The Cummington Story* [film]
		"Faure [sic] Festi-val at Harvard"	"Jubilee Variation on a Theme of Goossens" (later, *Variations on a Theme by Goossens*) [orch]
1946	Copland dated the beginning of his determination to learn to conduct	"Letters to Nicolas Slonimsky and to Arthur V. Berger"	*Billy the Kid*, arr. 2 pf [from ballet]
		"Neglected Works: A Symposium"	*Billy the Kid*, ex-cerpts arr. chamber orch [from ballet]
	Elected member of American Society of Composers, Authors, and Pub-lishers (ASCAP)		*Rodeo*, arr. pf [from ballet]
			"Hoe-Down" (from *Rodeo*), arr. string orch; arr. vn, pf [from ballet]

Year	Biography	Writings	Compositions
			Danzón Cubano, arr. of 2 pf piece [orch]
1947	Third Symphony awarded New York Music Critics' Circle outstanding orchestral work Toured South America sponsored by State Department, "practiced" conducting his own works	"Aaron Copland Writes from South America" "Benjamin Britten: *The Rape of Lucretia*, an Opera in Two Acts" "Composer's Report on Music in South America" "Influence, Problem, Tone" "Komponisten ohne Glorienschein" "Memorial to Paul Rosenfeld" "Nueva generatión de compositores norteaméricanos"	*Letter from Home*, arr. full orch [orch] Clarinet Concerto (1947–48) [orch] *Midsummer Nocturne* (1947/1977) [kb] *Four Piano Blues* (1947, 1926/1934, 1948, 1926) [kb] *In the Beginning* [chor]
1948		"The Art of Darius Milhaud" "South American Journey" "Eine neue amerikanische Komponistengeneration" "The New 'School' of American Composers" "Stefan Wolpe: Two Songs for Alto and Piano from *The Song of Songs*"	*The Red Pony* [film] *The Red Pony*, orch suite, 6 scenes [from film] *The Heiress* [film]

Year	Biography	Writings	Compositions
		Heylbut, Rose. "America Goes to the Ballet: A Conference with Aaron Copland" (I)	
1949		"A Modernist Defends Modern Music"	*Preamble for a Solemn Occasion* [orch]
		"Music and the Movies"	*Preamble for a Special Occasion* [orch]
		"The Personality of Stravinsky"	
		"Tip to Moviegoers: Take Off Those Ear-Muffs"	
		"What Is Jewish Music?: *The Music of Israel* by Peter Gradenwitz"	
		"The World of A-Tonality"	
1950	Oscar Award from the Academy of Motion Picture Arts and Sciences for best dramatic film score of *The Heiress*	"The American Musical Scene"	*Billy the Kid*, excerpts arr. vn, pf [from ballet]
		"Leon Kirchner: Duo for Violin and Piano"	Piano Quartet [cham]
		"Ralph Hawkes: In Memorium"	*Twelve Poems of Emily Dickinson* [song]
	Elizabeth Sprague Coolidge Foundation commissioned Quartet for Piano and Strings		*Old American Songs I* (arrs.): "The Boatmen's Dance," "The Dodger," "Long Time Ago," "Simple Gifts," "I Bought Me a Cat" [song]
	1950s: Involvements with dodecaphonic system		

Year	Biography	Writings	Compositions
1951	Fulbright Fellowship Revisited Europe for 6 months, and Israel for the first time Juilliard School of Music commissioned *Piano Fantasy* 1951–52: Charles Eliot Norton Professor of Poetry, Harvard, first composer to receive, leading to *Music and Imagination*	"L'america ha la sua música: Creare un'arte propria per una civilta' industriale" "Current Chronicle: United States, New York" "La musica moderna è nata in reazione a Wagner" "Problemes de la musique de film" "William Schuman: *String Quartet* no. 4"	
1952	Purchased first home—Shady Lane Farm—in Ossining, New York. Remained there 1952–61 League of Composers/Rodgers and Hammerstein commissioned television opera (*The Tender Land*) to celebrate the League of Composers' 30th anniversary	"The Gifted Listener" "An Indictment of the Fourth B" *Music and Imagination* "Tanglewood's Future: Measures to Insure Continuity Include Extensive New Scholarship Program" Nichols, Lewis. "Talk with Aaron Copland" (I)	*The Tender Land* (1952–54) [opera] *Billy the Kid*, excerpts arr. vc, pf [from ballet] *John Henry*, rev. full orch [orch] *Piano Fantasy* (1952–57) [kb] *Old American Songs II* (arrs.): "The Little Horses," "Zion's Walls," "The Golden Willow Tree," "At the River," "Ching-a-Ring Chaw" [song]
1953	Testified in secret session in McCarthy hearings	Brant, LeRoy V. "America, Involved in Music, Is Becoming Great in Music" (I) "Always in My Thoughts"	*Preamble for a Solemn Occasion*, arr. org [from orch]

Year	Biography	Writings	Compositions
		"Creativity in America"	
		"The Essence Remained"	
		"The Measure of Kapell"	
		"Music Out of Everywhere"	
		"*Notes Without Music*, by Darius Milhaud"	
1954	Elected to membership in the American Academy of Arts and Letters, eventually becoming president[1]	"Festival in Caracas: Recent Venezuelan Event Was Devoted to Composers of Latin America"	*The Tender Land*, rev. 3 acts [opera]
			Appalachian Spring, complete ballet, orch [from ballet]
		"[Letter to Music Editor]" *New York Times*, 4 October 1954	"The Promise of Living" (from *The Tender Land*) SATBB, pf duet [chor]
		"[Letter to Music Editor]: Letter from Composer"	"The Promise of Living" (from *The Tender Land*) arr. chorus, orch [chor]
		"Music: As an Aspect of the Human Spirit"	"Stomp Your Foot" (from *The Tender Land*) SATB, pf duet [chor]
		Taubman, Howard. "Copland's New Opera" (I)	"Stomp Your Foot" (from *The Tender Land*) arr. chorus, orch [chor]
			Old American Songs I, arr. v, orch [song]

[1] Other memberships or fellowships include Accademia di S. Cecilia, Royal Academy of Music, Royal Society of the Arts, Academia Nacional de Belles Artes (Buenos Aires), and University of Chile; he was director or board member of the American Music Center, American branch of the ISCM, Koussevitzky Foundation, Edward MacDowell Association, Charles Ives Society, and Naumburg Foundation and advisory editor of *Perspectives of New Music*.

Year	Biography	Writings	Compositions
			"Dirge in Woods" [song]
			"Laurie's Song" (from *The Tender Land*) [song]
1955		"Modern Music: 'Fresh and Different'"	*The Tender Land*, final rev [opera]
			Symphonic Ode, rev [orch]
			Canticle of Freedom [chor]
1956	Gold Medal of the American Academy of Arts and Letters	"American Culture I: Music, 1956" or "American Culture Series"	*Variations on a Shaker Melody* (from *Appalachian Spring*) [sym band]
	Honorary degree from Princeton University	"At the Thought of Mozart"	
	American conducting debut with Chicago Symphony at Ravinia Park	"The Dilemma of Our Symphony Orchestras"	
		"Report on American Music"	
		"Rubin Goldmark: A Tribute"	
		"Serious Music Serious Problems: Few Can Name the Tune"	
1957	*The World of Nick Adams* for television	"Fantasy for Piano: Composer Explains Its Particular Problems"	*The World of Nick Adams* (teleplay), orch [incd]
		"Piano Fantasy by Aaron Copland"	*Orchestral Variations* (arr. of *Piano Variations*) [orch]
		Copland, Aaron, and Jack Diether. "Guide to Record Collecting: Aaron Copland Suggests a Basic Mahler Library"	*Old American Songs II* arr. v, orch [song]

Year	Biography	Writings	Compositions
		Gräter, Manfred. "Aaron Copland Besucht Europa"	
1958		"Aaron Copland Talks about American Music Today" (I)	*The Tender Land*, orch suite [from opera]
		"Performers and New Music"	
		"Twentieth Century: Reorientation and Experiment"	
		"[A Visiting Composer]"	
		Gold, Don. "Aaron Copland: The Well-Known American Composer Finds Virtues and Flaws in Jazz" (I)	
1959	1959–72: Speaker, pianist, or conductor on 59 television programs	"American Composers on Records"	*Dance Panels* [ballet]
		"El compositor en los Estados Unidos"	*Dance Panels*, arr. 2 pf [from ballet]
		"Opera for America (Written for *Musik der Zeit*, Bonn)"	"Danza" (from *Three Latin-American Sketches*) arr. pf [from orch]
		The Pleasures of Music: An Address at the University of New Hampshire, April 16, 1959	
		Karsh, Yousuf. "Aaron Copland" (I)	
		Newman, Bill. "Aaron Copland" (I)	

Year	Biography	Writings	Compositions
1960	Purchased Rock Hill near Peekskill, remained there for rest of life Grammy Award for *The Tender Land Suite,* recorded by the Boston Symphony 1960s: Waning popularity with young composers, compositional career slows	"Classical or Modern: Aaron Copland Questions a Common Musical Distinction" (I) "America's Young Men of Music" "A Businessman Who Wrote Music on Sundays" "Composers and Composing" *Copland on Music* Foreword to *Portrait of a Symphony* "Four Weeks in the Soviet Union" "Making Music in the Star-Spangled Manner" "Nadia Boulanger: An Affectionate Portrait" "On Music Composition" "Oper für Amerika" "Search for an 'American' Music" "The Teacher: Nadia Boulanger" "A Tribute to Franz Liszt" "Visit to Peekskill" (I)	*Nonet* [cham]
1961	Honorary degree from Harvard University MacDowell Colony Medal	"The Composer as Critic" "Composing for *Something Wild*"	*Something Wild* [film]

Year	Biography	Writings	Compositions
	1961–68 President, Edward MacDowell Association	"On the Occasion of the 70th Birthday of Serge Prokofiev" "Six on the State of Music" (I)	
1962	September 23: *Connotations* premiered for opening of New York's Lincoln Center for the Performing Arts, televised live	"Composers in Russia" "A Composer's Praise" "Down a Country Lane" "Irving Fine (1914–1962)" "A Note on Irving Fine" "[Zoltán Kodály—80th Birthday]"	*Dance Panels*, rev. [ballet] *Letter from Home*, rev. chamber orch [orch] *Connotations* [orch] *Down a Country Lane* [kb]
1963		"Composers' Letters" "A Quarter-Century Reflection" "A Visit to Snape" Freeman, John W. "The Reluctant Composer: A Dialogue with Aaron Copland" (I)	"Danza" (from *Three Latin American Sketches*) arr. 2 pf [from orch]
1964	Received the Presidential Medal of Freedom for Peacetime Service, awarded by President Lyndon B. Johnson	"ASCAP and the Symphonic Composer" "Charles Ives" "Cousin Michael" "In Memory of Marc Blitzstein (1905–1964)"	*Music for a Great City* (from *Something Wild*) [orch] *Down a Country Lane* (arr. of pf piece) school orch [orch] *Emblems* [sym band]

Year	Biography	Writings	Compositions
*		"Music: My Way of Life" "Nadya Bulanzhe—Uchitel' Kompozitsii"	
1965	1965–66: Wrote, conducted, and hosted 12 programs, *Music in the 20s,* for National Educational Television	Burton, Humphrey. "The Art and Life of Aaron Copland" (I) "[Mellers, Wilfred Howard]" *Music in a New Found Land,* by Wilfred Howard Mellers [Book Review] "Musikalisches Schaffen in Amerika" "An Open Letter about the BBC from Aaron Copland" "Tributes and Reminiscences: Aaron Copland"	*Dance Panels,* arr. pf [from ballet] *Canticle of Freedom,* rev [chor]
1966		"The Contemporary Scene" "[Dmitri Shostakovich—60th Birthday]" "Irving Fine" "Letters to the Editor: *The Naked Image*"	*The Red Pony,* sym band suite, 4 scenes [from film] *In Evening Air* [kb]
1967	*Inscape* performed by New York Philharmonic Orchestra for 125th anniversary	"The Creative Mind and the Interpretive Mind"	CBS Playhouse, signature theme, brass, perc [incd]

Year	Biography	Writings	Compositions
	Honorary degree from Rutgers University	"Salute to the Arts and Artists of Latin America"	CBS Playhouse, signature theme, brass, perc [incd]
		"A Tribute to Nadia Boulanger"	*Variations on a Shaker Melody* (from *Appalachian Spring*) [orch]
		Szmolyan, Walter. "Gespräch mit Aaron Copland" (I)	*Inscape* [orch]
1968		Cone, Edward T. "Conversation with Aaron Copland" (I)	
		"Composer from Brooklyn: An Autobiographical Sketch"	
		"The Music of Chance"	
		The New Music, 1900–1960	
		"When Private and Public Worlds Meet"	
		Frymire, Jack. "Copland 68" (I)	
		Rorem, Ned. "Where Is Our Music Going?" (I)	
1969		"Aaron Copland: A Visit to Israel"	*Happy Anniversary* [orch]
		Foreword to *Thesaurus of Orchestral Devices*, by Gardner Read	*Inaugural Fanfare* [wind ens]
			Ceremonial Fanfare [brass]
		"International Music Congress—Forum"	
		"Kann ein Komponist vom Komponieren leben?"	

Year	Biography	Writings	Compositions
		"A Visit to Israel"	
		Mayer, William. "The Composer in the U.S. and Russia: A Frank Talk between Copland and Khachaturian" (I)	
1970	Awarded German Republic Commander's Cross of the Order of Merit Awarded Yale University's Henry Howland Memorial Prize	"Composers in the University" "Foreword to New Collection of 'The Gift to be Simple'" "In Memoriam 1945, Szeptember 26" "Is the University Too Much with Us?" Hamilton, David. "An Aaron Copland Photo Album" (I) Henahan, Donal. "He Made Composing Respectable Here" (I) Mayer, William. "Interview with Aaron Copland and Aram Khachaturian" (I) Soria, Dorle J. "Artist Life" (I)	*Eight Poems* arr. v, chamber orch (from *Twelve Poems of Emily Dickinson*) [from song]
1971		"The Role of the Composer/Le rôle du compositeur"	*Three Latin-American Sketches*: "Estribillo," "Paisaje Mexicana" (1959), "Danza de Jalisco" (1959) [orch]

Year	Biography	Writings	Compositions
		Cox, Ainslee. "Copland on the Podium" (I)	"Larghetto Pomposo" ("Happy Birthday") [brass]
			Duo [cham]
			Threnody I ("In Memoriam Igor Stravinsky") [cham]
1972	*Night Thoughts* composed for 1972 Van Cliburn International Piano Competition in Fort Worth, Texas	"In Memoriam Igor Stravinsky: Canons & Epitaphs—Set 2"	*Vocalise* (arr. of song), fl, pf [cham]
		"[Letter to Editor?] For the Record!"	*Vocalise* (arr. of song), ob, pf [cham]
		"[Letter to Editor], *New York Times*, 27 April 1972"	*Night Thoughts (Homage to Ives)* [kb]
		"[Letter to the Editor] Varèse"	
		"Piano Fantasy—Comments by Mr. Copland"	
		Ford, Christopher. "Copland, the Conductor" (I)	
		Valencia M., Ernesto. "Aaron Copland, el hombre, el musico, la leyenda" (I)	
1973	Essentially retired from composing; primarily conducting	Bessom, Malcolm E. "Conversation with Copland" (I)	*Preamble for a Solemn Occasion*, arr. sym band [from orch]
		"New Electronic Media"	*Threnody II* ("In Memoriam Beatrice Cunningham") [cham]
		Stevenson, Joe. "A Conversation with Aaron Copland" (I)	*Proclamation* (1973/1982) [kb]

Year	Biography	Writings	Compositions
1974		Bredemann, Dan. "Audience Is First—Copland" (I)	
		Preface to *Composers, Conductors, and Critics*, by Claire R. Reis	
1975	Interviews with Vivian Perlis began for autobiography	"Copyright Revision and the U.S. Symphonic Composer"	*Inaugural Fanfare*, rev [wind ens]
		"Night Thoughts"	
		Jones, Robert. "Aaron Copland: Musician of the Month" (I)	
		Kenyon, Nicholas. "The Scene Surveyed" (I)	
1976	Honorary degree from the University of Leeds in England	"The Life of Music"	"Nocturne" (from *Two Pieces*) arr. cl, pf [cham]
		"Music Is the Message"	
		Johnson, Harriett. "Aaron Copland: Dean of American Composers" (I)	
		"A Leading Composer Looks at American Music Today" (I)	
1977		"Aaron Copland on the ELP Version of *Fanfare for the Common Man*"	*Duo*, arr. vn, pf [cham]
		"Copland Salutes Boulanger"	

Year	Biography	Writings	Compositions
		Dickinson, Peter. *First American Music Conference, Keele University, England, April 18–21, 1975* (I)	
		Freedman, Guy. "A Copland Portrait" (I)	
1978	Awarded the American Symphony Orchestra League's Gold Baton	"Claire Reis (1889–1978)"	*Four Piano Blues*, nos. 1 and 2 arr. chamber orch (1978–79) [from kb]
		"Copland on Carter"	
		"In Appreciation . . . [Leonard Bernstein]"	
		Overton, James L. "It's a Very Lively Scene . . . We're in Good Shape" (I)	
1979	Awarded Kennedy Center Honors in Washington, D.C.	"None in the Same Way"	
		Davis, Dana. "A Copland Portrait" (I)	
		Rosenberg, Deena, and Bernard Rosenberg, "Aaron Copland" (I)	
1980	Already awarded 33 honorary degrees	Barnes, Patricia. "Aaron Copland on a Lifetime of Music" (I)	
		Caine, Milton A. "Comments on Copland" (I)	

Year	Biography	Writings	Compositions
		"More Comments on Copland"	
		"Orchestral Magic"	
		"Copland Recalls Criticism" (I)	
		Ramey, Phillip. "Copland and the Dance" (I)	
		Ramey, Phillip. "Copland at 80" (I)	
		Rosenwald, Peter J. "Aaron Copland Talks about a Life in Music" (I)	
		Rothstein, Edward. "Fanfares for Aaron Copland at 80" (I)	
		Silverman, Robert. "Aaron Copland: Happy Birthday" (I)	
		Smit, Leo. "A Conversation with Aaron Copland on His 80th Birthday" (I)	
1981		"Nadia Boulanger, Mother of Modern Music"	
		Hall, Roger. "An Interview with Aaron Copland" (I)	
		Hershowitz, Alan. "Aaron Copland: The American Composer Shares His Mind" (I)	

Year	Biography	Writings	Compositions
		Isacoff, Stuart. "Copland at 80: A Birthday Inter- view" (I)	
		Keener, Andrew. "*Gramophone* Perspective: Aaron Copland" (I)	
		Orga, Ates. "Aaron Copland Talks to Ates Orga" (I)	
1982	Aaron Copland School of Music founded at Queens College of the City University of New York	Foreword to *Stravinsky in Mod- ern Music (1924–1946)*	
		Gagne, Cole, and Tracy Caras. "Aaron Copland" (I)	
		Hall, Roger. "Aaron Copland— An Interview with Roger Hall" (I)	
1983	Essentially retired from conducting		Sonata for Violin and Piano, arr. cl, pf [cham]
1984		Copland, Aaron, and Vivian Perlis. *Copland: 1900 through 1942*	
		Copland, Aaron, and Vivian Perlis. "Looking Back with Aaron Cop- land"	
1985	Over 100 American musical organiza- tions celebrated his 85th birthday	"Aaron Copland on Aaron Cop- land"	

Year	Biography	Writings	Compositions
	July 24: Last public appearance at Aaron Copland Day celebration at Tanglewood with Leonard Bernstein conducting the Third Symphony		
1986	National Medal of Arts Congressional Gold Medal from House of Representatives	"Nadia Boulanger"	Sonata for Violin and Piano, rev [cham]
1987		"I Had a Great Deal to Learn . . ."	
1989		Copland, Aaron, and Vivian Perlis. *Copland: Since 1942*	
1990		"Grace Notes: Fortieth-Birthday Greeting to the Music Library Association from Aaron Copland, 1971" Hall, Roger. "Aaron Copland's 'Simple Gifts'" (I)	
1991	December 2: died in Tarrytown, New York	"Gabriel Fauré, a Neglected Master" Whyte, Bert. "Fanfare for an Uncommon Man" (I)	
2000	Copland 2000, a two-year celebration of the centenary of his birth, organized by Boosey & Hawkes, began		

Compositions With No Date
Appalachian Spring, suite, 13 instruments [from ballet]
pf trio (from Organ Symphony) [from orch]

Writings With No Date
"A. C. (A Composer) Looks at L. P."
"A. C.: Foreword to *Modern Music Reprints of Articles about I. Strav[insky]*"
"About *Billy the Kid*"
"As a Musician: Women's University Glee Club"
"The Battle of Jazz and the Classics"
"Claire Raphael Reis"
"The Composer and the Audience"
"The Composer as Conductor"
"The Composer in the United States"
"The Composer Speaks Out! Meet the Composer!"
"Contemporary Music—Is It Peculiar?"
"The Danger of Writing Concert Music"
"For Composers News Record"
"For the Record!" [Letter to Editor?]
"Franz Liszt"
"From a Composer's Journal"
"How We Listen"
"Intro[duction] to Claire Reis'[s] book, *Composers, Conductors and Critics*, 1974"
"Jak słuchać muzyki współczesnej" ("Listening to Contemporary Music")
"[Letter to Editor], *New York Times*"
"[Letter to Editor re: Olin Downes]"
"Miklós Rósza and Bernard Herrmann"
"Milhaud: First Symphony and *In Memoriam* (Columbia Album) and *Protée—Symphonic Suite No. 2* (Victor Album DM 1027)"
"Miscellany: Notes for Articles"
"Music for the Theatre"
"Music in America: Past, Present, and Future"
"Music in the Air"
"*The Music of Israel*, by Peter Gradenwitz, New York: W. W. Norton, Inc."
"La música como aspecto del espiritu humano"

"La musica per film: nuovo mezzo di espressione musicale"
"On Being a Composer"
"Outline of History (Nef)"
"Phonograph Recordings"
"Piano Music of Noël Lee"
"Portrait of a Symphony"
"Questions on Music"
"A Salute to Schwann"
"Sobre la música en el cine"
"Special Fondness for B. B. [Benjamin Britten]"
"Talk on N. B. [Nadia Boulanger]"
"U.S. Books and Music: A Vital and Varied Music"
"A Vital and Varied Music"
"Where Are We? What's Been Happening to So-Called Serious
   Music in the Sixties"
"The Youngest Generation of American Composers"
"Zoltán Kodály"

III. Primary Sources— Copland's Writings

A. Books and Essay Collections

1. *Copland on Music*. Garden City, NY: Doubleday, 1960. 280 p. ISBN 0393001989. ML63 .C48. (Reprint—New York: W. W. Norton, 1963. ML63 .C78 1963. Also Reprint—New York: Da Capo, 1976. 285 p. ISBN 0306707756. ML63 .C48 1976.)

Hoping to supply "historical perspective," Copland collected his individual essays and articles published elsewhere between 1926 and 1960 to "make more evident one composer's viewpoint." He hoped to stimulate the curiosity of young readers by "recapturing some of the excitement of those earlier days in the immediacy of impressions and reactions." Collectively, the essays illustrate the breadth of Copland's involvement in contemporary and American music. The chapters are all annotated separately as articles in Section III.B, except for "1959: Postscript for the Generation of the Fifties," which was first published in this collection. (See below.)

Contents *Copland on Music*

ACKNOWLEDGMENTS

FOREWORD

SECTION ONE:
1. Three Talks

The Pleasures of Music
        See: *The Pleasures of Music: An Address at the University of New Hampshire, April 16, 1959*
Creativity in America
        See: "Creativity in America"
Music as an Aspect of the Human Spirit
        See: "Music: As an Aspect of the Human Spirit"

2. Five Personalities
The Conductor: Serge Koussevitzky
        See: "Serge Koussevitzky and the American Composer"
The Teacher: Nadia Boulanger
        See: "Nadia Boulanger: An Affectionate Portrait"
The Composer: Igor Stravinsky
        See: "Influence, Problem, Tone" and "The Personality of Stravinsky"
The Critic: Paul Rosenfeld
        See: "Memorial to Paul Rosenfeld"
The Pianist: William Kapell
        See: "The Measure of Kapell"

3. Four Masters
At the Thought of Mozart
        See: "At the Thought of Mozart"
Berlioz Today
        See: "Berlioz Today" and "Composers and Composing"
Liszt as Pioneer
        See: "A Tribute to Franz Liszt"

4. From a Composer's Journal
        See: "From a Composer's Journal"

SECTION TWO:
The Twenties and the Thirties: How It Seemed Then
1. The Younger Generation of American Composers: 1926–59
1926: America's Young Men of Promise
        See: "America's Young Men of Promise"
1936: America's Young Men—Two Years Later
        See: "Our Younger Generation: Ten Years Later"
1949: The New "School" of American Composers

See: "The New 'School' of American Composers"
1959: Postscript for the Generation of the Fifties

2. European Festival and Premières: A Glance Backward:
Zurich: 1926
    See: "Playing Safe at Zurich"
Baden-Baden: 1927
    See: "Forecast and Review: Baden-Baden, 1927"
Paris: 1928
    See: "Stravinsky's *Oedipus Rex*"
London: 1931
    See: "Contemporaries at Oxford: 1931"
Berlin: 1932
    See: "Stravinsky and Hindemith Premieres"

3. The Composers of South America: 1941
    See: "The Composers of South America"

SECTION THREE:
The Reviewing Stand
1. Music By:
Darius Milhaud (1947)
    See: "The Art of Darius Milhaud"
Benjamin Britten (1947)
    See: "Benjamin Britten: *The Rape of Lucretia*, an Opera
    in Two Acts"
Stefan Wolpe (1948)
    See: "Stefan Wolpe: Two Songs for Alto and Piano from
    The Song of Songs"
Leon Kirchner (1950)
    See: "Leon Kirchner: Duo for Violin and Piano"
William Schuman (1951)
    See: "Current Chronicle: United States, New York"

2. Books About:
Virgil Thomson's Musical State (1939)
    See: "Thomson's Musical State"
Schönberg and His School (1949)
    See: "A World of A-Tonality"
The Life and Music of Bartók (1953)
    See: "The Essence Remained"

SECTION FOUR:
Occasional Pieces
1. "'Are My Ears on Wrong?': A Polemic"
     See: "Modern Music: 'Fresh and Different'"

2. Interpreters and New Music
     See: "Interpreters and New Music"

3. The Dilemma of Our Symphony Orchestras
     See: "The Dilemma of Our Symphony Orchestras"

4. Shop Talk: On the Notation of Rhythm
     See: "On the Notation of Rhythm"

---

2. *Music and Imagination.* Cambridge: Harvard University Press,
   1952. ix, 116 p. ISBN 0674589009 (cloth); 0674589157
   (paper). ML3853 .C7. (Reprint—New York: New American
   Library, 1959. 127 p. ML3853 .C7 1959.)

Music and Imagination is the text of Copland's six Charles Eliot
Norton lectures, presented between 1951 and 1952 at Harvard
University. Throughout the lectures, Copland examined the central
role of imagination in the creation and perception of music: "The
first half of the book treats of the musical mind at work in its different capacities as listener, interpreter, or creator. The second half discusses more specifically recent manifestations of the imaginative
mind in the music of Europe and the Americas." Chapters that are
annotated separately as articles in Section III.B are indicated below.

Contents *Music and Imagination*

PREFACE
INTRODUCTION
Part One: Music and the Imaginative Mind
"The Gifted Listener"
     See: "The Gifted Listener"
"The Sonorous Image"

"The Creative Mind and the Interpretive Mind"
   See: "The Creative Mind and the Interpretive Mind"
Part Two: Musical Imagination in the Contemporary Scene
"Tradition and Innovation in Recent European Music"
"Musical Imagination in the Americas"
"The Composer in Industrial America"
POSTSCRIPT

3. *The New Music, 1900–1960.* Rev. and enl. ed. New York: W. W. Norton, 1968. 194 p. ML197 .C76 1968.

This book, originally published in 1941 under the title *Our New Music; Leading Composers in Europe and America,* is comprised of Copland's article and lectures. Generally, Copland amended articles with postscripts from 1967 or footnotes correcting dated information. Occasionally he omitted text that was no longer appropriate. New chapters in *The New Music, 1900–1960* include the preface to the revised edition, "The Depression Years," "Dodecaphonic Developments," "Stravinsky's Conversion," and a revised "The Present Day." Chapters eliminated from *Our New Music; Leading Composers in Europe and America* include "The Present Day," "The Composer and Radio," "The World of the Phonograph," and "Music in Films." The chapters that are annotated separately as articles in Section III.B are indicated below. See: *Our New Music; Leading Composers in Europe and America.*

Contents *The New Music, 1900–1960*

PREFACE
PREFACE TO THE REVISED EDITION
ACKNOWLEDGMENTS

I. Survey of Contemporary European Composers (1900–1960)
The Argument
Preliminaries
The Background—Late Nineteenth Century
        Nationalism
        Moussorgsky's Realism
        The Impressionism of Debussy

The Late Romantics: Strauss, Mahler, Scriabin, Fauré,
Sibelius
    See: "Five Post-Romantics"
The Foreground—Before 1914
    Schoenberg's Expressionism
    Stravinsky's Dynamism
    Béla Bartók
Music between the Wars (1918–1939)
    Music after the First World War
    Ravel and Roussel
    Satie and "Les Six"
    The Lyricism of Milhaud
        See: "The Lyricism of Milhaud"
    The Jazz Interlude
        See: In part "Jazz Structure and Influence"
    The Neoclassic Movement
    The Neoclassic Influence
    The Depression Years
    Dodecaphonic Developments
    Stravinsky's Conversion

II. Composers in America
Composers without a Halo
    See: "Komponisten ohne Glorienschein"
New Music in the U.S.A.
    See: "The Composer in America, 1923–1933"
The Ives Case
    See: In part "One Hundred and Fourteen Songs"
Roy Harris
Sessions and Piston
Thomson and Blitzstein
    See: "Marc Blitzstein"
Composer from Mexico: Carlos Chávez
    See: "Carlos Chávez—Mexican Composer"
Composer from Brooklyn: An Autobiographical Sketch
    See: "Composer from Brooklyn" and "Composer from
    Brooklyn: An Autobiographical Sketch"

III. The Present Day
The Generation of the Fifties

4. *Our New Music; Leading Composers in Europe and America.*
New York: McGraw-Hill, 1941. xiv, 305 p. ML197 .C76 N5.

This is the original text that was revised and enlarged as *The New Music, 1900–1960* in 1968. Copland discussed contemporary music in the United States and Europe, contextualizing it with observations about nineteenth-century music. The chapters that are annotated separately as articles in Section III.B are indicated below. See: *The New Music, 1900–1960.*

Contents *Our New Music; Leading Composers in Europe and America*

PREFACE
ACKNOWLEDGMENTS

I. Survey of Contemporary European Composers
The Argument
Preliminaries
The Background—Late Nineteenth Century
      Nationalism
      Moussorgsky's Realism
      The Impressionism of Debussy
      The Late Romantics: Strauss, Mahler, Scriabin, Fauré, Sibelius
        See: "Five Post-Romantics"
The Middle Ground—Before 1914
      Schoenberg's Expressionism
      Stravinsky's Dynamism
      Béla Bartók
The Foreground—Since 1918
      Music after the First World War
      Ravel and Roussel

Satie and "Les Six"
The Lyricism of Milhaud
   See: "The Lyricism of Milhaud"
The Jazz Interlude
   See: In part "Jazz Structure and Influence"
The Neoclassic Movement
The Neoclassic Influence
The Present Day
   See: In part "The Musical Scene Changes"
Coda

II. Composers in America
Composers without a Halo
   See: "Komponisten ohne Glorienschein"
New Music in the U.S.A.
   See: "The Composer in America, 1923–1933"
Personalities
   The Ives Case
    See: In part "One Hundred and Fourteen Songs"
   Roy Harris
   Sessions and Piston
   Thomson and Blitzstein
    See: "Marc Blitzstein"
Composer from Mexico: Carlos Chávez
   See: "Carlos Chávez—Mexican Composer"
Composer from Brooklyn: An Autobiographical Sketch
   See: "Composer from Brooklyn" and "Composer from
   Brooklyn: An Autobiographical Sketch"

III. New Musical Media
The Composer and Radio
The World of the Phonograph
   See: "The World of the Phonograph"
Music in the Films
   See: "Second Thoughts on Hollywood"
APPENDIX
INDEX

5. *What to Listen for in Music.* New York: McGraw-Hill, 1939. xiii, 281 p. MT6 .C78W4. (Reprint—New York: New American Library, 1953. 159 p. MT6 .C78W4 1953. Also Reprint—Rev. ed. New York: McGraw-Hill, 1957. 307 p. MT6 .C78 1957. Also Reprint—With an introduction by William Schuman. New York: McGraw-Hill, 1988. xxiv, 307 p. ISBN 0070130914. MT6 .C78W4. Also Reprint—With a foreword and epilogue by Alan Rich, introduction by William Schuman. New York: Mentor, 1999. xxxii, 266 p. ISBN 0451628802. MT6 .C78W4 1999.)

In this book Copland instructed listener-readers in the elements and forms of music. The content was drawn from fifteen lectures that Copland presented at the New School for Social Research in New York, during the winters of 1936 and 1937. His goal was to "put down as clearly as possible the fundamentals of intelligent music listening" for the layperson and music student. Written from the perspective of a composer, rather than an educator, Copland explained: "The composer has something vital at stake. In helping others to hear music more intelligently, he is working toward the spread of a musical culture, which in the end will affect the understanding of his own creations." Copland's educational philosophy is a reflection of his larger musical philosophy: "I have tried to apply every point made not only to established masterworks but also to the music of living men." Chapters 16 and 17 were added for the 1957 edition. Chapters that are annotated as separate articles in Section III.B are indicated below.

CONTENTS *What to Listen for in Music*

INTRODUCTION
AUTHOR'S NOTE FOR THE 1957 EDITION
PREFACE
ACKNOWLEDGMENTS
1. Preliminaries
2. How We Listen
    See: "How We Listen"
3. The Creative Process in Music
    See: "The Creative Process in Music"
4. The Four Elements of Music—I. Rhythm

6. Copland, Aaron, and Vivian Perlis. *Copland: 1900 through 1942.* New York: St. Martin's/Marek, 1984. xii, 402 p. ISBN 0312169620. ML410 .C756 A3 1984.

Until 1999, *Copland: 1900 through 1942,* based on interviews by Vivian Perlis with the composer and his associates, represented the most exhaustive autobiography/biography of Copland. The book alternates contextual "Interlude" chapters and interviews with Copland's associates, written by Perlis, with discussions by Copland of his life and compositions. The book is easily readable, with Copland's sections giving a glimpse at his personality. Although Copland discussed every composition in chronological order, detailing biographical and compositional influences, there is no theoretical analysis of the compositions.

The first volume ends with a discussion of *Fanfare for the Common Man*.

7. Copland, Aaron, and Vivian Perlis. *Copland: Since 1942.* New York: St. Martin's Press, 1989. xii, 463 p. ISBN 0312033133. ML410 .C756 A3 1989.

The second volume of Copland's autobiography/biography continues the format of the first volume, beginning with Copland's score for the film *The North Star*. Perlis took a more active role in narrating this second volume, which includes seven "Interlude" sections, alternating with nine chapters based on interviews with Copland.

B. Articles and Essays

1. Copland as Sole Author

8. "A.C. (A Composer) Looks at L.P." n.d. MS. 197/1, Aaron Copland Collection. Music Division, Library of Congress, Washington, DC.

In this incomplete handwritten manuscript, Copland notes that composers, as "individuals or as a professional group," had yet to address the "new dimensions" that the long-play record had added to composition.

9. "A.C.: Foreword to *Modern Music Reprints of Articles about I. Strav[insky].*" n.d. MS. 197/2, Aaron Copland Collection. Music Division, Library of Congress, Washington, DC.

See: Foreword to *Stravinsky in Modern Music (1924–1946).*

10. "Aaron Copland: A Visit to Israel." *Boosey and Hawkes Newsletter,* 3 (Spring 1969): 1.

Copland conducted the Israel Philharmonic in a program of twentieth-century works (Charles Ives, Igor Stravinsky, and Copland) during 1968. In addition to reporting on the reception of the program by audience and orchestra, Copland describes the musical superstructure in Israel, observing that much had been accomplished since his first visit in 1951. Copland lists current Israeli composers, noting their move away from "interest in local-color composition," as well as gains in organization and "compositional self-confidence." See: "A Visit to Israel."

11. "Aaron Copland on Aaron Copland." *The Instrumentalist,* 4 (November 1985): 66–69.

This article is a transcription of comments excerpted from a television show (WQED/Pittsburgh) called "A Copland Celebration." In the article, Copland briefly discusses topics such as the use of jazz in the 1920s to create a recognizably American voice, *El Salón México, A Lincoln Portrait, A Fanfare for the Common Man, Appalachian Spring,* composing for films, conducting and Leonard Bernstein, and music education in the United States.

12. "Aaron Copland on the ELP Version of *Fanfare for the Common Man.*" *Contemporary Keyboard,* 3 (October 1977): 30.

This is a one-paragraph justification by Copland of his decision to allow Emerson, Lake & Palmer, "a gifted group," to record their own version of *Fanfare for the Common Man.* As Copland points out, since he held the copyright, there was "something that attracted [him]" to their version, or else he would not have granted his permission.

13. "Aaron Copland Writes from South America." *Tanglewood Alumni Bulletin,* 1 (Autumn 1947): 3–4.

Writing from Rio de Janeiro, Copland reports on the activities of the United States Group for Latin American Music and of Eleazar de Carvalho, conductor of the Orquestra Sinfonica Brasileira. Copland summarizes his involvement with Carlos Chávez and Mexican music, predicting that music in South America would develop similarly to music in Mexico. The current musical environment in Brazil was similar to that in the United States "some thirty or forty years ago," but conditions remained uneven among South American countries and cities.

14. "About *Billy the Kid.*" n.d. MS. 197/6, Aaron Copland Collection. Music Division, Library of Congress, Washington, DC.

Reflecting upon the twelfth anniversary of the premiere of *Billy the Kid,* Copland writes, "Whatever else one might think, I suppose that Billy started a trend since it was the first of the ballet westerns. Certainly it was the first time that I attempted to tap the rich source of American folk music and give it a full orchestral setting." In addition to the genesis and scenario of *Billy the Kid,* Copland discusses the challenges of harmonizing and orchestrating a folk tune.

15. "Active Market in New Music Records." *Modern Music,* 13 (January–February 1936): 45–47.

In this article, Copland reviews current releases by RCA-Victor, Columbia, and New Music Quarterly Recordings, commenting on composers, compositions, and performances (often by the composers themselves). He documents the growing but anonymous market for modern music recordings and the current state of recording technology in which string quartets sounded best, choral works worst, and tempi and "breaks" during compositions were compromised by the length of a single record. The advent of the phonograph "provides the acid test—a piece must 'have something' if it will withstand repeated playing."

16. "The Aims of Music for Films." *New York Times,* 10 March 1940, sec. 11, p. 7.

In this article, Copland reflects on the scoring in *Of Mice and Men,* which he had recently completed, and on the state of musical composition for films. He takes exception to the prevailing practice of writing mediocre film scores "in the lush tradition of the nineteenth century," despite the period depicted by the film. He also argues the assumption that "the better a motion picture score is, the less attention it attracts," stating instead that quality film scores should be promoted, just like high-profile directors. Quoting Virgil Thomson, Copland states that the purpose of film scores is to bridge "the gap between the screen and the audience."

17. "Always in My Thoughts." *Perfect Home Magazine,* February 1953, p. 3.

Although "still ahead," Copland's perfect home had been "always in [his] thoughts." After recounting past residences, Copland describes his perfect home as "easy to leave, and delightful to come back to," with a piano in its main room ("not one of those new-fangled spindly things, but a rich-toned, vibrant instrument, whose mere presence induces music").

18. "L'america ha la sua musica: Creare un'arte propria per una civiltà industriale." *La fiera letteraria, Settimanale delle lettere delle arti e delle scienze,* 6 (4 March 1951): 1, 7.

This article is taken in part from "The American Musical Scene" and like that article is aimed at validating American music for the European. See: "The American Musical Scene."

19. "The American Composer Gets a Break." *American Mercury,* 34 (April 1935): 488–492.

Although 1934 was a banner year in the establishment of an American art music, American composers still did not receive the same serious consideration as writers and artists. Refuting the argument that the American composer was "without character," Copland enumerates the accomplishments of four eminent composers in their thirties—Roy Harris, Roger Sessions, Virgil Thomson, and Walter Piston. The American composer will not occupy "a genuine and natural place in society; not merely . . . tolerated and encouraged, but needed" until an audience with "an active appetite" for contemporary music has been created.

20. "The American Composer Today." *U.S.A.: An American Review,* 2 (1945): 23–27.

As a result of the increase in stature of American music and the influx of European composers living in the United States, Copland predicted that the "future of European music will be closely allied with the course which music takes in the Americas." Although Native American chants, Anglo-Saxon songs, African American spirituals, and jazz provided an early inspiration for American composers, "none has proved to be the final and conclusive solution to the problem of an original and recognizable *American* style in music." A more lasting definition of Americanness in music has emerged as "a love of big frescoes, of broad and simple outlines, and a certain nervous energy and rhythmic incisiveness." Surveying the past fifteen years, Copland chronicles the contributions that he, Roy Harris, William Schuman, George Gershwin, and Bernard

Herrmann made in the genres of opera, film, radio, ballet, chamber, and orchestral music. See: "American Music since 1930."

21. "American Composers on Records." 1959. MS. 197/13, Aaron Copland Collection. Music Division, Library of Congress, Washington, DC.

This is the manuscript for the somewhat abbreviated "U.S. Books and Music: A Vital and Varied Music." See: "U.S. Books and Music: A Vital and Varied Music."

22. "American Culture I: Music, 1956" or "American Culture Series."

(Written for the Associated Press, this article was picked up by at least thirty-seven different newspapers, under various titles, with differing amounts of editing and pictures depending on available space.) Despite the development of a "vital school" of American composers over the previous thirty years, "serious" music did not receive the same recognition as literature and the other arts. Attempting to correct public perception, Copland states that American art music composers need the same musical superstructure that existed in Europe—"an organized musical community . . . that includes piano manufacturers as well as competent teachers, cultivated audiences and plenty of concert activity." Admonishing the audience to "get to know" American music, Copland demonstrates its richness, chronicling the institutional structure, composers, and compositions representative of symphonic music, opera, dance, film, and jazz. See: "American Culture I: Music, 1956," "Report on American Music, 1956," "Serious Music Serious Problem: Few Can Name the Tune," "El compositor en los Estados Unidos," and "The Composer in the United States."

23. "American Music since 1930." 1945. MS. 197/15, Aaron Copland Collection. Music Division, Library of Congress, Washington, DC.

This is a typescript draft, dated July 1945, for "The American Composer Today." See: "The American Composer Today."

24. "The American Musical Scene." *Olympia: Journal der musikalischen Wettkämpfe,* 1 (May 1950): 50.

Because of Europe's "cultural hegemony," Europeans are reluctant to consider the United States "among the world's leading musical creators." Significant American composers have been slow to develop because of the lack of an established superstructure in the United States—performers, publishers, critics, and networks of financial support. American composers, however, have benefited from broad exposure to international music and the democratization of music through radio, television, phonograph, and film. Copland then categorizes American composers by age: those in their fifties (Roy Harris, Roger Sessions, Walter Piston, Virgil Thomson, Howard Hanson, and George Gershwin), those approaching forty (William Schuman, Samuel Barber, Marc Blitzstein, and David Diamond), and those still in their twenties and early thirties (Harold Shapero, Leon Kirchner, Alexei Haieff, Lukas Foss, Leonard Bernstein, Robert Palmer, and William Bergsma).

25. "America's Young Men of Music." *Music and Musicians*, 9 (December 1960): 11, 33.

In this article, originally a lecture on American music given in London, Copland surveys the compositional contributions and influences of the "younger American composers." He divides them as follows: Elliott Carter (First String Quartet and his use of rhythmic modulation), a Boston School (including Harold Shapero, Lukas Foss, Irving Fine, Arthur Berger, and Leonard Bernstein), a "Juilliard School" (Peter Mennin, William Bergsma, and Vincent Persichetti), and a California School (Leon Kirchner and Andrew Imbrie). Copland both praises and questions Gunther Schuller's combination of "progressive" jazz with classical music and John Cage's compositional use of silence, chance, and the prepared piano. He concludes that the musical scene, while "lively," is not unified. See: "A Businessman Who Wrote Music on Sundays," "Making Music in the Star-Spangled Manner," and "Search for an 'American' Music."

26. "America's Young Men of Promise." *Modern Music*, 3 (March–April 1926): 13–20. (Reprint—"1926: America's Young Men of Promise." In *Copland on Music*.)

Invoking the names of Franz Liszt, Erik Satie, Ferruccio Busoni, Arnold Schoenberg, and Alfredo Casella, who had championed young European composers, Copland laments the lack of such figures in the United States. Copland surveys the careers of seventeen composers, between the ages of twenty-three and thirty-three, and groups them into schools—Prix de Rome, Revolutionaries, Free Lances, Students of Ernest Bloch, and Students of Nadia Boulanger. Copland discusses the merits and shortcomings of selected works by Howard Hanson, George Antheil, Henry Cowell, Roger Sessions, Roy Harris, Douglas Moore, and Virgil Thomson.

27. "America's Young Men—Ten Years Later."

See: "Our Younger Generation Ten Years Later."

28. "Are My Ears on Wrong? A Reply to Mr. Henry Pleasants" and "'Are My Ears on Wrong?': A Polemic."

See: "Modern Music: 'Fresh and Different.'"

29. "The Art of Darius Milhaud." *Saturday Review,* 26 June 1948, p. 43. (Reprint—"Darius Milhaud [1947]." In *Copland on Music.*)

In this article, Copland outlines the historical and musical highlights of Darius Milhaud's First Symphony, *In Memoriam,* and *Protée—Symphonic Suite No. 2.* He muses on the general public's "curious lack of vocal enthusiasm in regard to Milhaud's music," although in Copland's opinion Milhaud was the most important French composer since Maurice Ravel. Copland was impressed by Milhaud's "markedly personal style," his "singing quality," and his "apparently inexhaustible productive capacity." See: "Milhaud: First Symphony and *In Memoriam* (Columbia Album) and *Protée—Symphonic Suite No. 2* (Victor Album DM 1027)."

30. "As a Musician: Women's University Glee Club." In *Gerald Reynolds: A Memorial.* Compiled and edited by Amy Groesbeck and Ella Levis, p. 33. New York: Rappaport Press, n.d.

This memorial was written for Gerald Reynolds (1886–1947). As a conductor of the Women's University Glee Club in the late 1920s, Reynolds had invited composers to write works specifically for the chorus, setting an example for later conductors. Reynolds also encouraged Copland to write his first compositions for women's voices—"The House on the Hill" and "An Immorality."

31. "ASCAP and the Symphonic Composer." *New York Times,*
    16 February 1964, sec. 11, advertisement, p. 10.

The American Society of Composers, Authors, and Publishers
(ASCAP) has played an important role in the protection of the composer's rights through the collection of fees on for-profit performances. Copland states: "All talk about a cultural awakening in
our country will have a hollow ring unless we can balance it with a
real concern for the well-being of our present-day creative musician. The body of work our composers create each year represents a
national asset, and should be protected as such."

32. "At the Thought of Mozart." *High Fidelity,* 6 (January 1956):
    53. (Reprint—In *Copland on Music.*)

Copland muses on composers' reactions to the music of Mozart,
stating that the more complex a twentieth-century composer, the
more the composer admired (and needed) Mozart. Considering
himself more critical than others, Copland likes Mozart best when
he has the sensation of watching him think. Reflecting on Paul
Valéry's definition of beauty as "that which makes us despair,"
Copland describes his "despair" upon hearing Mozart's music as
"the realization that only this one man at this one moment in musical history could have created works that seem so effortless and so
close to perfection."

33. "Baden-Baden, 1927."

See: "Forecast and Review: Baden-Baden, 1927" and "European
Festivals and Premieres: A Glance Backward."

34. "The Battle of Jazz and the Classics." n.d. MS. 197/22, Aaron
    Copland Collection. Music Division, Library of Congress,
    Washington, DC.

These are brief handwritten notes in which Copland explores the
mutual relationship between jazz (read swing and "popular" music)
and classical music. He writes: "It is legitimate for classical music to
borrow from popular sources—Always has been done . . . But it is a
sign of degeneracy for popular music not to be able to invent its
own melodic treatment." He concludes that art music does not need
to be popularized or legitimized by swing music renditions.

35. "Benjamin Britten (1947)."

See: "Benjamin Britten: *The Rape of Lucretia,* an Opera in Two Acts."

36. "Benjamin Britten: *The Rape of Lucretia,* an Opera in Two Acts." *Music Library Association Notes,* 2d ser., 4 (March 1947): 190–191. (Reprint—"Benjamin Britten [1947]." In *Copland on Music.*)

In reviewing the piano-vocal score for Benjamin Britten's chamber opera, *The Rape of Lucretia,* Copland pronounces it better than Britten's first opera, *Peter Grimes*—an important trajectory, since Britten was still in his early thirties. Copland assesses Britten's compositional talents, including his "richness of melodic invention," which was unlike the speech rhythms set by Marc Blitzstein or Virgil Thomson.

37. "Berlin: 1932."

See: "European Festivals and Premieres: A Glance Backward" and "Stravinsky and Hindemith Premieres."

38. "Berlioz Today."

"Berlioz Today" from *Copland on Music* was published in a somewhat abbreviated form in "Composers and Composing." See: "Composers and Composing."

39. "Blashfield Address: Creativity in America."

See: "Creativity in America."

40. "A Businessman Who Wrote Music on Sundays." *Music and Musicians,* 9 (November 1960): 18, 33.

In this article—transcribed by the United States Information Service from a talk on American composers given in London—Copland discusses four composers who had rejected the idea of writing identifiably American-sounding music: Roger Sessions and Walter Piston, as representatives of composers then in their early sixties, and William Schuman and Samuel Barber, as representatives of composers in their early fifties. Such composers argued that approaching music as anything but a "universal art" was "demeaning to the composer." Copland also discusses Charles Ives's compositional influence for Americans as the "first composer who was anxious in some way to connect the music that he was writing with the sort of life that he knew." Copland also promotes the vision of Ives as an incomplete genius, "living in a sort of waste land." See: "America's Young Men of Music," "Making Music in the Star-Spangled Manner," and "Search for an 'American' Music."

41. "Carlos Chávez—Mexican Composer." *New Republic*, 54 (2 May 1928): 322–323. (Reprint—In *American Composers on American Music: A Symposium*. Edited by Henry Cowell, 102–106. Stanford: Stanford University Press, 1933. ML200.5 C87 A5. Also Reprint—New York: F. Ungar, 1962. xiv, 226 p. ML 200.5 .C87 A5 1962.)

In this article, Copland heralds the presence of Carlos Chávez, a "thoroughly contemporary composer" whose work was "one of the first authentic signs of a new world with its own [non-European] music." By way of explaining Chávez's "modern" music, Copland enumerates the differences between late Romantic and contemporary music. He discusses the Mexican "Indian" influence on Chávez's work, stating that no other composer using folk material had "more successfully solved the problem of its complete amalgamation into an art-form." This article was later updated as "Composer from Mexico: Carlos Chávez" in *Our New Music* and *The New Music*.

42. "Charles Ives." 1964. MS. 197/25, Aaron Copland Collection. Music Division, Library of Congress, Washington, DC.

This biography of Charles Ives, which includes now-standard biographical information, is especially interesting from the standpoint of Copland's evaluations, both positive and negative, of Ives's compositions: "The unusually imaginative way in which these disparate and often banal elements are embedded in the texture of his music accounts in part for the originality of his musical style." And "his major problem as composer was to find formal coherence, especially in larger works." Copland's typescript includes the notation "Written for the American People's Encyclopedia."

43. "Claire Reis (1889–1978)." *Musical Quarterly*, 64 (July 1978): 386–388.

This is an extremely personal and anecdotal tribute to Claire Reis at her death. Copland describes Reis—former chair of the board of the League of Composers, promoter of Copland's music, and close friend for over fifty years—as "an energetic champion of living composers." Among her most "formidable" assets were her high energy, "innate dynamism," and leadership. Since Copland rarely discussed women in the musical superstructure, it is interesting to note that his description of Reis's career is interspersed with accounts of Reis as a "devoted wife, mother, sister, aunt—as well as a cordial host."

44. "Claire Raphael Reis." n.d. MS. 197/27, Aaron Copland Collection. Music Division, Library of Congress, Washington, DC.

Copland wrote this essay, which he labeled "Unfinished and unused article about Claire Raphael Reis," shortly after her death. Among Reis's accomplishments Copland noted her support of living composers, her position as chair of the League of Composers, and her publication *Composers in America*. Copland quoted at length from William Schuman's introduction to the 1977 reissue of Reis's text, in which Schuman credited Reis with being an "ideal patron." Neither Copland nor Schuman was able to describe Reis without mentioning her personality, family, or the social gatherings at her home.

45. "The Composer and His Critic." *Modern Music*, 9 (May–June 1932): 143–147. (Reprint—*Perspectives of New Music*, 2 [Spring–Summer 1964]: 22–23.)

Because of docile audiences in the United States, American critics hold more influence than European critics. Among American critics' additional responsibilities should be a concern with the creation of an American music. They should acquaint themselves with recent American music by talking to composers, rather than being dependent on a conductor's programming. This article includes important documentation of Copland's developing American aesthetic and his views on the cultural health of the country. The article in *Perspectives of Music* is an abridged version of the article in *Modern Music*.

46. "The Composer and the Audience." n.d. MS. 198/2, Aaron Copland Collection. Music Division, Library of Congress, Washington, DC.

In this one-page typescript, written sometime after 1930, Copland reflects on the preoccupation of composers of Ludwig van Beethoven's era with form, of Frédéric Chopin's era with harmony, and of the first two decades of the twentieth century with technical innovations. Following a period of revolutionary experimentation (1900–1930) that alienated audiences, Copland felt that contemporary composers' foremost concern was the reaction of the audience.

47. "The Composer as Conductor." n.d. MS. 198/3, Aaron Copland Collection. Music Division, Library of Congress, Washington, DC.

See: "When Private and Public Worlds Meet."

48. "The Composer as Critic." *Graduate Comment* [Wayne State University], 5 (October 1961): 23–25.

Speaking from the perspective of "a composer in his capacity as critic," Copland enumerates four types of criticism that a composer practices: criticism of his or her own composition, of the interpreter of the compositions, of the musical critic, and of contemporary society. Composers critique themselves in the act of composing, since every compositional choice implies critical consideration of one musical element over another. The composer critiques the musical frame of reference applied to a composition by the interpreter. An ideal critic can supply an important perspective on a creative artist's work and should be a participant in the musical culture, as opposed to solely a "reporter of events." As a social critic, the composer expresses in a permanent and beautiful form "what it feels like to be alive now in these United States."

49. "Composer from Brooklyn." *Magazine of Art,* 32 (September 1939): 522–523, 548–550. (Reprint—"Composer from Brooklyn: An Autobiographical Sketch." In *Our New Music.* Also Reprint—"Aaron Copland: Composer from Brooklyn." In *The American Composer Speaks: A Historical Anthology, 1770–1965.* Edited by Gilbert Chase, pp. 167–177. Baton Rouge: Louisiana State University Press, 1966. ix, 318 p. ML 90 .C55.)

This article is a standard source of information on Copland's musical education and career through *Billy the Kid* and *Our Town.* He begins this autobiographical sketch with the often-quoted sentences

"I was born on a street in Brooklyn that can only be described as drab . . . Music was the last thing anyone would have connected with it." Copland traces his pre-Paris musical training, his studies with Nadia Boulanger, and his increasing recognition following his return to the United States. This article is also the source of Copland's references to the absence of women composers and composition teachers in art music. The reprinted "Aaron Copland: Composer from Brooklyn" includes an additional three-paragraph biographical introduction to Copland.

50. "Composer from Brooklyn: An Autobiographical Sketch." In *The New Music, 1900–1960.* (Reprint—*ASCAP Today,* 2 [Winter 1968]: 4–8.)

Copland revised and enlarged "Composer from Brooklyn" (*Our New Music*) into "Composer from Brooklyn: An Autobiographical Sketch" (*The New Music, 1900–1960*). In the 1967 postscript that Copland created for *The New Music, 1900–1960,* he takes exception to being solely categorized by outdated comments ("I wished 'to see if I couldn't say what I had to say in the simplest possible terms'"), made in the late 1930s, which led to his works being dichotomized as "serious" or "popular." He discusses at length "the fervent years" of the 1930s, his composition of *Appalachian Spring,* his career as a conductor, his involvement with Tanglewood, and his use of twelve-tone compositional techniques. The article in *ASCAP Today* is excerpted from *The New Music.*

51. "Composer from Mexico—Carlos Chávez."

See: "Carlos Chávez—Mexican Composer."

52. "The Composer: Igor Stravinsky."

See: "Influence, Problem, Tone" and "The Personality of Stravinsky."

53. "The Composer in America, 1923–1933." *Modern Music,* 10 (January–February 1933): 87-92. (Reprint—"New Music in the U.S.A." In *Our New Music* and *The New Music.*)

At the end of World War I, modern music became an organized movement in the United States, gaining a somewhat reluctant acceptance between 1923 and 1933. That decade marked the introduction of radio broadcasting, the system of the guest conductor, an influx of new music, and the eventual recognition of New York City as an international musical center. Copland recounts a lengthy history of the beginnings of American contemporary music, characterizing the period from 1923 to 1933 as a "chaotic state of musical values." He predicts that the following decade will be an assimilation of the previous experiments, with audience and composer moving closer together. Copland lists both (1) a younger and (2) an older generation of male composers active during the 1920s, and (3) a subsequent generation of nine composers—including only one woman—all of which constituted an "American school of composers." [(1) Ernest Bloch, John Alden Carpenter, Louis Gruenberg, Charles Ives, Frederick Jacobi, Harold Morris, Leo Ornstein, Carl Ruggles, Carlos Salzedo, Lazaro Saminsky, Edgard Varèse, Emerson Whithorne; (2) George Antheil, Nicolai Berezowsky, Marc Blitzstein, Carlos Chávez, Copland, Henry Cowell, Howard Hanson, Roy Harris, Colin McPhee, Dane Rudhyar, Roger Sessions, Leo Sowerby, William Grant Still, Virgil Thomson, Randall Thompson, Bernard Wagenaar; and (3) Henry Brant, Paul Bowles, Israel Citkowitz, Lehman Engle, Vivian Fine, Irwin Heilnew, Bernard Herrmann, Jerome Moross, and Elie Siegmeister.] Copland revised this article for inclusion in *Our New Music* by updating his lists of influential composers and conductors. The chapter in *Our New Music* was then reprinted, with an additional 1967 postscript, in *The New Music, 1900–1960*. In the postscript, Copland contradicts his earlier prediction that "new music in the future will no longer be confined to the sphere of the special society."

54. "The Composer in the United States." n.d. MS. 198/7, Aaron Copland Collection. Music Division, Library of Congress, Washington, DC.

This is a partial handwritten draft in English for "El compositor en los Estados Unidos." See: "El compositor en los Estados Unidos" and "Serious Music Serious Problem: Few Can Name the Tune."

55. "The Composer Speaks Out! Meet the Composer!" n.d. MS. 198/8, Aaron Copland Collection. Music Division, Library of Congress, Washington, DC.

Copland tells of a meeting with a schoolboy who was incredulous that composers were living people. In a flourishing musical culture, the living composer should be placed at the beginning, rather than the end, of a list of musical institutions: "conductors . . . then opera singers and child prodigies, instrumental virtuosi, first-rate orchestras, endowed conservatories, etc." It is "highly symptomatic of our [unhealthy] entire musical set-up" that living composers are such a curiosity (even for adults). See: "The Live Composer."

56. "Composers and Composing." *Saturday Review,* 27 August 1960, p. 33–35.

In these excerpts from *Copland on Music,* Copland attributes the contemporary interest in Hector Berlioz to "the quality of emotion in his music—the feeling of romanticism classically controlled— that reflects one aspect of present-day sensibility." Berlioz's music could appear "both remote in time and then suddenly amazingly contemporary." The article also includes short paragraphs in which Copland commented on the compulsion to compose opera, Maurice Ravel as an orchestrator, Arnold Schoenberg as an interpreter, and the struggle of literary authors to articulate thoughts about music. See: "Berlioz Today" and "From a Composer's Journal."

57. "The Composers Get Wise." *Modern Music,* 18 (November–December 1940): 18–21.

Reviewing the relatively new performance fees for copyrighted material, Copland calls for "total collection—which means that each time a piece is played in public 'for profit' a performance fee should be collected." Speaking for a growing number of composers, Copland states "that only through . . . the *collection of monies directly derived from the music they compose,* will the creative artists in this country be able to produce a maximum amount of music." Copland compares how the copyright laws differ when applied to popular and art music performances, recordings, and publications.

58. "Composers in the University." 1970. MS. 198/14, Aaron Copland Collection. Music Division, Library of Congress, Washington, DC.

This is the typescript for "Is the University Too Much with Us?" See: "Is the University Too Much with Us?"

59. "Composers in Russia." *Boston Symphony Orchestra* Bulletin (1961–1962): 100–108. MT125 .B66.

In the spring of 1962, Copland and Lukas Foss traveled in the Soviet Union, conducting, performing, lecturing on radio, and observing performances of folk music and jazz. Copland notes that
"comparatively little recent Western music" was being heard live in
the Soviet Union, causing even young, controversial composers to
write in a pervasively Russian aesthetic, comparable to Sergei
Prokofiev's *Scythian Suite.* Copland reports that no level of dissonance surprises the Russians, despite "active propaganda on the
part of those in a position of authority to discredit 12-tone atonal-
ism and what was referred to as 'electronic noises' when composed
as absolute music." Copland calls for a similar exchange of Russian
music and composers with the United States, especially of the
younger generation, several members of which he lists. (According
to a note in the *Boston Symphony Orchestra Bulletin,* this article is
reprinted from the *New York Herald Tribune* on 8 May 1962; however, the original publication was not found there.) See: "Four
Weeks in the Soviet Union."

60. "Composers' Letters." *Musical America,* 83 (January 1963): 14.

Copland wrote this brief letter to Claire Reis in 1951, while he was
in residence at the American Academy in Rome. He compares the
Santa Cecilia concerts, founded in 1566 by Palestrina, to concerts
by the League of Composers.

61. "The Composers of South America." *Modern Music,* 19 (Jan-
    uary–February 1942): 75–82. (Reprint—"The Composers of
    South America: 1941." In *Copland on Music.*)

In this article, somewhat revised and updated for *Copland on Music,*
Copland addresses the state of South American music, stressing that
because of the diversity between and within countries there is no
typical South American composer. Yet all South American composers work under serious handicaps of an underdeveloped musical
superstructure of orchestras, radio broadcasts, publishing, and education. For each country discussed (particularly Argentina, Brazil,
and Chile), Copland highlights the status of musical organizations,
regional folk musics, national aesthetics, and individual composers.

62. "A Composer's Praise." *The Justice* [Brandeis University], 30
    October 1962, 7. (Reprint—*Boston Symphony Orchestra*
    Bulletin [December 1962]: 645–646. MT125 .B66.)

This is a short eulogy for Irving Fine—composer, teacher, and per-former. Describing Fine's compositions, Copland states that they all "'sound'; they have bounce and thrust and finesse; they are always a musical pleasure to hear." Fine's real legacy, however, lay in his musicianship: "His outstanding quality was his musical sensitiv-ity—he had an ear that one could trust. His students and his fellow composers depended on him to tell the truth about their music and, in general, about the music of our time." (Unable to confirm Cop-land's citation for the *Boston Symphony Orchestra* Bulletin.) See: "A Note on Irving Fine."

63. "Composer's Report on Music in South America." *New York Times,* 21 December 1947, sec. 2, p. 9.

As part of a cultural exchange under the aegis of the Department of State, Copland toured major cities and small northern coastal towns in Brazil, conducting five concerts and lecturing in public and on radio. From Bahia and Recife, he reports on an instrument called the berimbau, on the frevo dance and its musical accompaniment, and on the performance of samba by Dorival Cayme, "Brazil's finest composer in the popular style." Copland notes that Brazilians were familiar with the names of American composers, primarily through radio broadcasts, rather than live performances or record-ings. He lists various Brazilian composers, including Camargo Guarnieri, Luis Gianneo, José María Castro, and Alberto Gi-nastera, "worth anybody's time." See: "South American Journey."

64. "Composers without a Halo."

See: "Komponisten ohne Glorienschein."

65. "Composing for *Something Wild.*" 1961. MS. 198/18, Aaron Copland Collection. Music Division, Library of Congress, Washington, DC.

Following a twelve-year hiatus, Copland returned to film composi-tion with the score for *Something Wild.* Although some of his ob-servations are specific to this film, there is a general discussion of cinematic compositional process including the evaluation of a film script, the importance of title music at the beginning of the film, and special considerations when setting music for an urban backdrop, an incoherent character, or an ambiguous relationship.

66. "El compositor en los Estados Unidos." *Buenos Aires Musical,* 14 (December 1959): 19–21.

This article, shortened and adapted for Latin American audiences, is a translation of "Serious Music Serious Problem: Few Can Name the Tune." In the new introduction to this article, Copland states that in 1941 North and South Americans knew comparatively little of each other's music. Only two decades later, however, the current Latin American composer had more in common with the North American composer than the European composer. See: "The Composer in the United States" and "Serious Music Serious Problem: Few Can Name the Tune."

67. "The Conductor: Serge Koussevitzky."

See: "Serge Koussevitzky and the American Composer."

68. "Contemporaries at Oxford: 1931." *Modern Music,* 9 (November–December 1931): 17–23. (Reprint—"London: 1931." In *Copland on Music.*)

In this article, shortened for *Copland on Music,* Copland is especially critical of the ninth annual International Society for Contemporary Music festival, held in Oxford and London. He writes: "Having won its cause, it no longer represents exclusively the most revolutionary tendencies in music, but exists rather to consecrate the glory of established reputations and to call to the attention of an international public the music of certain newer composers." Among the works Copland reviews are pieces by Roman Palester, Wladimir Vogel, Anton Webern, Vladimir Dukelsky, Constant Lambert, Juan José Castro, Fernand Quinet, Virgilio Mortari, George Gershwin, Karol Szymanowski, Ferenc Szabó, Ralph Vaughan Williams, Albert Roussel, Lev Knipper, Jan Maklakiewicz, Ernesto Halffter, Roger Sessions, Jean Huré, Egon Wellesz, Eugene Goossens, Józef Koffler, Otto Jokl, Paul Hindemith, and Erwin Schulhoff.

69. "Contemporary Music."

See: "A Modernist Defends Modern Music."

70. "Contemporary Music—Is It Peculiar?" n.d. MS. 198/20, Aaron Copland Collection. Music Division, Library of Congress, Washington, DC.

This is the typescript for "A Modernist Defends Modern Music." The chapter "Contemporary Music" in *What to Listen for in Music* and "A Modernist Defends Modern Music" are essentially the same. See: "A Modernist Defends Modern Music," "Jak słuchać muzyki współczesnej," and "Contemporary Music" in *What to Listen for in Music*.

71. "The Contemporary Scene." *Saturday Review,* 25 June 1966, p. 49.

This article is taken from remarks delivered at the fiftieth-anniversary Pulitzer Prize Dinner in May 1966, at which Copland was asked to "sort out trends" in music. Copland cautions the musically conservative, saying that "we are living in the midst of an unprecedented musical revolution," as the result of "the injection of science and scientific calculation." With the advent of computers and their resultant changes to music, "it is too much to expect that so-called normal music will remain just as it was in the past." Copland then categorizes avant-garde music as either highly controlled or unpredictable, both of which ultimately can sound similar.

72. "Copland on Carter." *Lincoln Center Stagebill* [Lincoln Center for the Performing Arts], 6 (November 1978).

In a brief assessment of Elliott Carter's work, Copland describes the composer as an "original creator . . . in the forefront of our leading creative writers." Carter's music "presupposes a listener with a sophisticated musical ear" and "continues to intrigue both the ear and the intellect after repeated hearings." Copland concludes that Carter's "independence, after all, is at the basis of his musical gift, and it is what gives added stature to our entire compositional scene."

73. "Copland Salutes Boulanger." *New York Times,* 11 September 1977, sec. 2, p. 25.

In this tribute, Copland credits Nadia Boulanger with inspiring in him "confidence in [his] own creative powers" and with encouraging the "specifically American rhythmic life in [his] music." Copland describes Boulanger's Wednesday afternoon classes for advanced students, followed by tea with a "cross-section of the composing community" of 1920s Paris, as "one of the stimulating aspects of studying with Mademoiselle." He concludes that Boulanger "acted as a musical godmother to an unusual number of gifted young people, and made each one of them aware of their own potential powers."

74. "Copyright Revision and the U.S. Symphonic Composer." *ASCAP Today,* 7 (Winter 1975): 9.

Always a defender of the art music composer's right to make a living from composing, Copland testified on behalf of the American Society of Composers, Authors, and Publishers (ASCAP) before a subcommittee of the Judiciary Committee of the U.S. House of Representatives. Copland proposed revisions to the "obsolete and inequitable" U.S. Copyright Act of 1909, recommending "an end to the juke box exemption, establishment of a tribunal that could review the juke box license fees in the future, and an extension of the copyright term."

75. "Cousin Michael." 1964. MS. 198/24, Aaron Copland Collection. Music Division, Library of Congress, Washington, DC.

This is the typescript for "Tributes and Reminiscences: Aaron Copland." See: "Tributes and Reminiscences: Aaron Copland."

76. "The Creative Mind and the Interpretive Mind." In *Music and Imagination.* (Reprint—In *Contemporary Composers on Contemporary Music.* Edited by Elliott Schwartz and Barney Childs, pp. 146–159. New York: Holt, Rinehart and Winston, 1967. Also Reprint—New York: Da Capo Press, 1978. ISBN 0306775875. ML197.S33 1978.)

In comparing the creative and interpretive minds, Copland concludes that their difference is the ability to conceive and shape "abstract ideas in extended forms." He reasons circularly that the lack of great women composers suggests that women's minds fall into the interpretive, rather than creative category. Copland describes creative inspiration as a "hallucinatory state of mind" driven by the artist's need "to make evident one's deepest feelings about life."

While the performer, a liaison between composer and audience, strives for "elocutionary eloquence," the composer wants stylistic interpretations "true for the composer's period and individual personality." Copland questions the existence of a national character in musical interpretation, concluding that while American orchestras possess a "live sound and . . . vitality in performance," they lack the straightforward naturalness of European orchestras.

77. "The Creative Process in Music." In *What to Listen for in Music.* (Reprint—"How the Composer Works." In *The Music Lover's Handbook.* Edited by Elie Siegmeister, pp. 59–65. New York: W. Morrow, 1943. xiii, 817 p. ML55 .S6. Also Reprint— In *The Meaning in Reading.* Edited by Jacob Hooper Wise, J. E. Congleton, Herman E. Spivey, and Alton C. Morris. Rev. ed., pp. 210–15. New York: Harcourt, Brace, 1947. 372 p. PR1363 .W55 1947. Also Reprint—In *The New Music Lover's Handbook.* Edited by Elie Siegmeister, pp. 43–46. New York: Harvey House, 1973. 620 p. ISBN 0817851518. ML55 .S62.)

Although the layperson assumes inspiration is of primary concern to the composer, for the composer—a trained professional—ability is the primary issue, while inspiration "is often only a by-product" of composition. Copland identifies four types of compositional inspiration as spontaneous, constructive, traditional, or experimental. Copland then describes the compositional process from the inception of the musical idea to how the composer assesses the theme for formal beauty and possible metamorphoses, how the appropriate sound medium is established, how subsidiary materials are created, and how the components are welded together to achieve *la grande ligne.*

78. "Creativity in America." In *Proceedings of the American Academy of Arts and Letters and the National Institute of Arts and Letters,* 2d ser., 3 (1953): 33–40. New York: Spiral Press, 1953. (Reprint—In *Copland on Music.*)

While the creative act is as basic to civilization as religious experience, the human and aesthetic implications of creativity are not evident to most Americans. Copland argues that since Americans undervalued art and the artist, creativity in the United States differed from other countries. Because "commercial and scientific knowledge" alone do not "justify a civilization," Americans must become "fully cognizant of the civilizing force that the work of art represents—a civilizing force that is urgently needed in our time."

While acknowledging that "bureaucratic control of the arts" is frightening, Copland believes that federal and state governments should support the arts as "free-lance patronage . . . is now becoming more inadequate each year." See: "Musikalisches Schaffen in Amerika."

79. "The Critic: Paul Rosenfeld."

See: "Memorial to Paul Rosenfeld."

80. "Current Chronicle: United States, New York." *Musical Quarterly,* 37 (July 1951): 394–396. (Reprint—"William Schuman [1951]." In *Copland on Music.*)

In a review of William Schuman's String Quartet No. 4, Copland stated that the work's "hermetic quality—this somewhat forbidding and recalcitrant aspect" presaged "an enlargement of the capacities of the William Schuman we know." Copland summarizes, "This is music written with true urgency: compact in form, ingenious in its instrumental technique, quite experimental as to harmony." He then discusses in depth each of the musical elements previously mentioned. See: "William Schuman: String Quartet no. 4."

81. "The Danger of Writing Concert Music." n.d. MS. 198/27, Aaron Copland Collection. Music Division, Library of Congress, Washington, DC.

This is a handwritten list of the musical and narrative elements to be considered when turning film music into a concert suite. Among the issues are "losing the bass," "curious importance and unimportance of detail," "importance of orchestral color," "use of the overlap" between tracks, "music as background atmosphere," and differences in melodic interest, orchestration, and phrasing.

82. "Darius Milhaud (1947)."

See: "The Art of Darius Milhaud."

83. "Defends the Music of Mahler."

See: "Letter on Gustav Mahler" and "[Letter to the Editor] Defends the Music of Mahler."

84. "The Dilemma of Our Symphony Orchestras." *Musical Courier,* 154 (1 November 1956): 6, 39. (Reprint—In *Copland on Music.*)

In this reprint of an address delivered to the American Symphony Orchestra League Convention, Copland calls for "proper representation of contemporary music on symphony programs." Many composers fear bringing their new symphonic compositions before musically undernourished audiences who have become used to programs that are "limited in scope, repetitious in content, and therefore unexciting." Among the dangers of the underrepresentation of living American composers is a lack of civic pride, the stifling of creativity of young composers, a lack of foresight for the future health of symphonies, and an unresponsiveness to listening tastes of the record-buying public. Copland calls for adequate variety in programming, a deliberately challenging element in each concert, and the development of new compositional talent as a "permanent feature of basic policy."

85. "*Discoveries of a Music Critic,* by Paul Rosenfeld" [Book Review].

See "Pioneer Listener."

86. "[Dmitri Shostakovich—60th Birthday]." 1966. MS. 198/31, Aaron Copland Collection. Music Division, Library of Congress, Washington, DC.

In this handwritten note, written on behalf of the "whole American musical public," Copland wishes Dmitri Shostakovich greetings on his sixtieth birthday. During the 1930s and the 1940s, Shostakovich showed "how one could speak of serious matters in a musical language that had a marked profile and a wide appeal."

87. "Down a Country Lane." *Life,* 52 (29 June 1962): 44–45.

This is the printed score of the piece for young pianists.

88. "The Essence Remained." Review of *The Life and Music of Béla Bartók* by Halsey Stevens. *New York Times,* 3 May 1953, sec. 7, pp. 7, 22. (Reprint—"The Life and Music of Bartók [1953]." In *Copland on Music.*)

Copland reviews *The Life and Music of Béla Bartók,* by Halsey Stevens, composer, critic, and head of the Music Department at the University of Southern California. Copland laments that the book is highly technical and focuses on analysis rather than biography. He is particularly enthusiastic about Stevens's description of Bartók's melding of folk materials with "modern" harmony and his "organic" development of two- and three-note motives—compositional concepts Copland valued.

89. "European Festivals and Premieres: A Glance Backward." 1960. MS. 198/32, Aaron Copland Collection. Music Division, Library of Congress, Washington, DC.

This is the typescript for the *Copland on Music* chapter "European Festivals and Premières: A Glance Backward," which includes "Zurich: 1926," "Baden-Baden: 1927," "Paris: 1928," "London: 1931," and "Berlin: 1932." See: "Zurich: 1926," "Playing Safe at Zurich," "Baden-Baden: 1927," "Forecast and Review: Baden-Baden, 1927," "Paris: 1928," "Stravinsky's *Oedipus Rex,*" "London: 1931," "Contemporaries at Oxford: 1931," "Berlin: 1932," and "Stravinsky and Hindemith Premieres."

90. "Fantasy for Piano: Composer Explains Its Particular Problems." *New York Times,* 20 October 1957, sec. 2, p. 9. (Reprint—"Piano Fantasy." In *Tempo,* 46 [Winter 1958]: 12–14.)

In this brief article, written prior to the premiere of *Piano Fantasy,* Copland reflects on the compositional difficulties associated with writing both a fantasy and an extended single movement, quoting at length from Paul Valéry. As if anticipating criticism of the work, Copland addresses the "tendency in recent years to typecast [him] as primarily a purveyor of Americana in music." He also justifies his combination of the twelve-tone method and tonality in the *Piano Fantasy,* stating that "twelve-tonism is nothing more than an angle of vision." See: "Piano Fantasy by Aaron Copland" and "Piano Fantasy—Comments by Mr. Copland."

91. "Fauré Centennial in America: 1945."

See: "Faure [sic] Festival at Harvard."

92. "Faure [sic] Festival at Harvard." *New York Times*, 25 November 1945, sec. 2, p. 4. (Reprint—"Fauré Centennial in America: 1945." In *Copland on Music*.)

Copland announces that the Harvard University Music Department is sponsoring five concerts to celebrate the hundredth anniversary of Gabriel Fauré's birth. Copland fears that Fauré's music might not be well received because the world chaos of the time was incongruous with Fauré's "restraint and classic sense." In general, Fauré's "Frenchness" had not translated well outside France. Copland discusses Fauré's aesthetic, stating that most people only knew several of the composer's works, all written before he was forty-five, but that all of Fauré's mature works were composed in the subsequent three decades.

93. "Festival in Caracas: Recent Venezuelan Event Was Devoted to Composers of Latin America." *New York Times*, 26 December 1954, sec. 2, p. 9.

Copland reports on the first-ever festival of orchestral works by contemporary Latin American composers, which featured forty symphonic compositions from seven Latin American countries. The festival was organized by Heitor Villa-Lobos, Carlos Chávez, Juan José Castro, and Rios Reyna. Copland observes that Villa-Lobos and Chávez were the two most prominent composers in Latin America. He critiques the programming for its overemphasis on "folk-inspired" South American genres, its underrepresentation of Chile, and its lack of experimental compositions. He also reviews compositions by Villa-Lobos, Chávez, Castro, and Julián Orbón.

94. "Film Music."

See: "Tip to Moviegoers: Take Off Those Ear-Muffs."

95. "Five Post-Romantics." *Modern Music*, 18 (May–June 1941): 218–224.

This article, edited for a musical readership, is taken from *Our New Music*. Although aesthetically a part of the nineteenth century, the music of Richard Strauss, Gustav Mahler, Alexander Scriabin, Gabriel Fauré, and Jan Sibelius contained musical elements (harmony, contrapuntal texture, orchestral timbre, and melodic line) that the twentieth-century composer "disengaged and utilized for new ends." Copland discusses Mahler's uniqueness, contrapuntal texture, and economic instrumentation; Strauss's modernistic harmonies; Scriabin's quartal harmonies and germinal ideas; and Sibelius's folk inspiration and mosaiclike use of motives. Copland's fondness for Fauré (Nadia Boulanger's teacher) stemmed from Fauré's essentially French temperament with its "harmonic sensibility, impeccable taste, classic restraint, and a love of clear line and sound proportion." See: "The Late Romantics: Strauss, Mahler, Scriabin, Fauré, Sibelius" in *Our New Music* and *The New Music.*

96. "For Composers News Record." n.d. MS. 199/1, Aaron Copland Collection. Music Division, Library of Congress, Washington, DC.

In this two-page typescript, Copland reports that South American music was "not as good as it's going to be, but it's already much better than you think it is." The influence between South and North American composers could be mutual, with North American composers learning from the incorporation of nationalistic and folkloric elements in the music of South America (especially Brazil, Argentina, and Chile). Conversely, the United States could offer assistance in publication and performances, in much the same way that France offered leadership to American composers between 1920 and 1935. While Latin American countries were isolated from Europe, the United States, and each other, there was some solidarity in national organizations such as the Liga de Compositores de la Argentina and the Grupo Renovación in Cuba.

97. "For the Record! [Letter to Editor?]." n.d. MS. 199/2, Aaron Copland Collection. Music Division, Library of Congress, Washington, DC.

See: "[Letter to Editor?] For the Record!," "[Letter to Editor], *New York Times,* 27 April 1972," and "[Letter to the Editor] Varèse."

98. "Forecast and Review: Baden-Baden, 1927." *Modern Music,* 5 (November-December 1927): 31–34. (Reprint—"Baden-Baden: 1927." In *Copland on Music.*)

The 1927 festival of *Deutsche Kammermusik,* held at Baden-Baden, featured chamber opera compositions, a relatively new genre written specifically for reduced forces of singers and instrumentalists. Copland assesses both the careers of and contributions to the genre of chamber opera by Darius Milhaud (*The Abduction of Europa*), Kurt Weill (*Mahagonny*), Paul Hindemith (*Hin und zurück*), and Ernst Toch (*The Princess on the Pea*). Copland also reports on performances of works by Alban Berg, Béla Bartók, and Hans Eisler, written for mechanical instruments, motion pictures, or chamber ensembles. See: "European Festivals and Premieres: A Glance Backward."

99. Foreword to *Portrait of a Symphony*. By Constantine Manos. New York: Basic Books, 1960. unpaged. ML87 .M36.

This foreword was written to accompany a book of photographs and text by Constantine Manos, celebrating the eightieth anniversary of the Boston Symphony Orchestra. The collection of photographs gave Copland the same impression that he had as a composer when he heard his own compositions played solely for him by a great orchestra. Manos captured the true life of an orchestra: the power and grace of the orchestra in performance, balanced by the "mundane scenes" of "back-stage preparations, the dramas of the tuning room, the gossip of the corridors, the gathering of the audience out front." See: "Portrait of a Symphony."

100. Foreword to *Stravinsky in Modern Music (1924–1946)*. Compiled by Carol J. Oja. New York: Da Capo Press, 1982. xix, 176 p. ISBN 0306761084. ML410 .S932S793 1982.

Igor Stravinsky's compositions during the second quarter of the twentieth century, with their "repeated sharp, unexpected turns in . . . musical style continually baffled composers, critics, and listeners." While European writers reacted to Stravinsky's music with apprehension and suspicion, Americans were more receptive, "uninhibited" by European traditions. According to Copland, Stravinsky's ability to "mix his elements, including even the familiar ones" in a sustained, unpredictable way "profoundly affected the course of music in our time." See: "A.C.: Foreword to *Modern Music Reprints of Articles about I. Strav[insky]*."

101. Foreword to *Thesaurus of Orchestral Devices,* by Gardner Read. New York: Greenwood Press, 1969. xxi, 631 p. ISBN 0837118840. MT70 .R37 1969.

Copland states that Gardner Read's *Thesaurus of Orchestral Devices,* a contemporary manual of orchestration, is unique in its exploration of "the subtle art of combining instruments." Modern composers could profit from the *Thesaurus*—a "compendium" of published orchestral excerpts—by perusing examples of colleagues' "ingenuity and coloristic imaginings." Similarly, students could examine the whole field of orchestration through the copious orchestral illustrations.

102. "Foreword to New Collection of 'The Gift to Be Simple.'"
     1970. MS. 199/4, Aaron Copland Collection. Music Division,
     Library of Congress, Washington, DC.

In this brief foreword written for (but not published in) the second edition of Shaker tunes by Edward D. Andrews (*The Gift to Be Simple: Songs, Dances, and Rituals of the American Shakers*), Copland expresses his long-term admiration for Andrews. It was through Andrews's first collection of Shaker tunes, *The Gift to Be Simple,* that Copland became acquainted with "Simple Gifts," which he set in his ballet *Appalachian Spring.* Copland describes the musical aesthetic and rhythmic structure that had attracted him to Shaker tunes.

103. "Four Weeks in the Soviet Union." 1960. MS. 198/13, Aaron
     Copland Collection. Music Division, Library of Congress,
     Washington, DC.

One draft for "Composers in Russia" is labeled "Four Weeks in the Soviet Union." See: "Composers in Russia."

104. "Franz Liszt." n.d. MS. 199/5, Aaron Copland Collection.
     Music Division, Library of Congress, Washington, DC.

See: "A Tribute to Franz Liszt."

105. "From a Composer's Journal." n.d. MS. 199/6, Aaron Copland Collection. Music Division, Library of Congress, Washington, DC.

This chapter of *Copland on Music* is essentially "Composers and Composing" with the deletion of "Berlioz Today" and the addition of "In Baden-Baden" (addressing Copland's desire to write an orchestrational extravaganza), "The Orchestral Musician" (who is uninvolved in the musical community), "Tempi" (an instinct for correct tempi is the most essential quality for a conductor), "Voices" ("I hate an emotion-drenched voice"), "The Young Conductor" (the difficulty of judging young conducting talent off the podium), and "Musical Arousal" (one can become aroused reading about music, just as with reading about sex). See: "Composers and Composing" in *Copland on Music.*

106. "From a Composer's Notebook." *Modern Music,* 6 (May–June 1929): 15–19. (Reprint of Stravinsky excerpt—*Stravinsky in Modern Music [1924–1946].* Compiled by Carol J. Oja, pp. 17-18. New York: Da Capo Press, 1982. xix, 176 p. ISBN 0306761084. ML410 .S932S793 1982.)

This article is a series of short contemplations on a variety of subjects. For his first topic, Copland questions the interpretation of the term "neo-classic" as "Back to Bach," particularly as it was applied to Piotr Tchaikovsky's influence on Igor Stravinsky's *Le baiser de la fée.* In "The American Composer Again," Copland argues that the weakness of American music was in its relatively young musical superstructure. Copland also considers the contributions of Mahler, the "pernicious" influence of Italian critic Ernest Newman, the "naturalness" of Virgil Thomson's speech setting in *Four Saints in Three Acts,* the contributions of "worthless" modern compositions, and the difference between masterpieces by Richard Wagner and Stravinsky or Arnold Schoenberg.

107. "From the Mail Pouch: The Composers Ob[ject]: A Response from Eleven Who Were Represented at Critics' Concerts [Letter to Editor]."

See: "[Letter to Editor] From the Mail Pouch: The Composers Ob[ject]: A Response from Eleven Who Were Represented at Critics' Concert" and "[Letter to Editor re: Olin Downes]."

108. "From the '20's to the '40's and Beyond." *Modern Music,* 20 (January–February 1943): 78-82.

In chronicling the advances that first occurred in American music during the 1920s and 1930s, Copland asserts that "we have come a particularly long way." For the first time composers began to earn their major income from composition, increasing the need for strict enforcement of copyright and royalty protections, and the federal government became involved in the sponsorship of music through the Depression–era Works Progress Administration. Young composers, now rivaling their elders "in technical dexterity," took an increasingly functional approach to their music. The "most startling" innovations of the past decades were the result of radio broadcasting and improved phonograph recordings, which created a new audience and challenged the conventional composer-audience relationship.

109. "Gabriel Fauré, a Neglected Master." *Musical Quarterly,* 10 (October 1924): 573–586.

In addition to the introduction annotated in the following citation, Copland conducted an extensive overview of Gabriel Fauré's compositions by genre—the piano compositions, chamber works, his single opera, and the songs that Copland particularly admired. Copland's mastery of Fauré's entire oeuvre is impressive; his praises for Fauré indicate Copland's musical values at the time.

110. "Gabriel Fauré, a Neglected Master." *Musical Quarterly,* 75 (Fall 1991): 48–50.

This is a reprint of primarily the introduction to Copland's 1924 article. Calling him "the Brahms of France," Copland champions Gabriel Fauré—Nadia Boulanger's teacher—as "the greatest living French composer," surpassing even Maurice Ravel and Florent Schmitt. Fauré did not enjoy this reputation outside France in part because of his Frenchness, which did not translate outside the country and because the most important of his works were composed after he was fifty, when he had been "safely shelved" by older critics and passed over in favor of Claude Debussy by younger critics.

111. "George Antheil." *League of Composers' Review (Modern Music),* 2 (January 1925): 26–28.

Copland wrote this article to clarify George Antheil's "real personality," which had been "cleverly concealed by a welter of words" from writers such as Ezra Pound and Antheil himself. Copland considered Antheil naive, youthful, sincere, and a born musician, despite "his lack of a natural feeling for form." Although struggling under the shadow of Igor Stravinsky to find his own personal idiom, Antheil possessed an "enviable future."

112. "The Gifted Listener." *Saturday Review,* 27 September 1952, 41, 43–44, 57. (Reprint excerpt—*Christian Science Monitor,* 29 June 1976, 21.)

In this excerpt from "The Gifted Listener," in *Music and Imagination,* Copland theorizes the differences between professional and amateur listening, ultimately concluding that both listeners respond to music on a "brutish level." While listening is a talent we all possess, the actual skill of listening can be developed. Copland states "The ideal listener, it seems to me, would combine the preparation of the trained professional with the innocence of the intuitive amateur." Contrasting two opposing views on the semantics of music's meaning, he concludes that the topic is "one of the thorniest problems in esthetics." See: "The Gifted Listener" in *Music and Imagination.*

113. "Grace Notes: Fortieth-Birthday Greeting to the Music Library Association from Aaron Copland, 1971." *Music Library Association Notes,* 2d ser., 46 (June 1990): 1093.

This nine-measure musical manuscript was written as a "salute" to the Music Library Association on its fortieth anniversary.

114. "How the Composer Works."

See: "The Creative Process in Music."

115. "How We Listen." n.d. MS. 199/10, Aaron Copland Collection. Music Division, Library of Congress, Washington, DC.

This article, which appears to have been published as an excerpt, is the same as the chapter in *What to Listen for in Music.* In it, Copland hypothesizes that there are three planes of musical listening: "1) the sensuous plane, 2) the expressive plane, 3) the sheerly musical plane." On the sensuous plane, the listener listens simply for the "sheer pleasure of the musical sound itself." The expressive plane is more complicated to discuss because the meaning of music—if it can even be agreed to have meaning—is subjective and difficult to

verbalize. Listening consciously to the musical elements of composition constitutes listening on the musical plane. Ultimately, listeners should strive for a more active listening, which will deepen their
understanding of music. See: "How We Listen" in *What to Listen
for in Music.*

116. "I Had a Great Deal to Learn . . . " *Keyboard Classics,* 7
    (March–April 1987): 9.

In this article, drawn from *Copland: 1900 through 1942* by Copland and Vivian Perlis, Copland describes his compositional technique for scoring *Of Mice and Men.* The article is an important
catalog of compositional decisions and constraints placed on the
Hollywood composer during the late 1930s and early 1940s.

117. "In Appreciation . . . [Leonard Bernstein]." *Stagebill* [Na-
    tional Symphony Orchestra], 25 August 1978, n.p.

In this brief letter, written for Leonard Bernstein's sixtieth birthday
concert, Copland states that Bernstein was the most "natural-born
musician" in the history of American music. Although the term
"'uniquely gifted' has been overused . . . in Leonard Bernstein's
case it truly has meaning."

118. "In Memoriam Igor Stravinsky: Canons & Epitaphs—Set 2."
    Tempo, 98 (1972): 22–23.

Copland's twenty-one measure manuscript score for flute, violin,
viola, and cello entitled "Threnody—Igor Stravinsky: In Memoriam" joins musical tributes to Stravinsky by Elliott Carter, Roger
Sessions, Darius Milhaud, Alexander Goehr, and Pierre Boulez.

119. "In Memoriam 1945, Szeptember 26." *Musika,* 13 (Septem-
    ber 1970): 7.

This is Copland's tribute to Béla Bartók at his death. (The citation is
not verified.)

120. "In Memory of Marc Blitzstein (1905–1964)." *Perspectives of
    New Music,* 2 (Spring–Summer 1964): 6–7. (Reprint ex-
    cerpt—"Marc Blitzstein Remembered." In *Philharmonic Hall,*

Lincoln Center for the Performing Arts Bulletin, 1963–1964,
p F.)

Copland laments that the present generation of musicians "has
little sense of who [Marc Blitzstein] was and what he accomplished." Blitzstein, self-described as "'addicted to the theatre,'"
wrote human drama, fueled by a "moral fervor." Influenced by
Bertold Brecht and Kurt Weill, Blitzstein helped establish a truly
American opera: "He was the first American composer to invent a
vernacular musical idiom that sounded convincing when heard
from the lips of the man-in-the-street."

121. "An Indictment of the Fourth B." *New York Times,* 21 September 1952, sec. 6, pp. 18, 59–60; *Music Journal,* 10 (November 1952): 13, 30–34; *Music Journal,* 22 (March 1964):
29, 86–89.

In this article, a portion of "The Gifted Listener" in *Music and
Imagination,* Copland criticizes current orchestral programming,
arguing that giving the audience only what it wants has led to "a
monotony of repertoire." (In the decade between 1940 and 1950,
forty percent of the symphonic repertoire in the United States was
composed of works by Ludwig van Beethoven, Johannes Brahms,
Wolfgang Amadeus Mozart, Richard Strauss, Piotr Ilyich
Tchaikovsky, and Richard Wagner.) Like life, a healthy musical culture "must be able to renew itself with fresh impetus from each new
generation of creators." The "standardization of repertoire," "rev-
erence for the classics," overemphasis of the interpreter's role, and
artists who ignore contemporary music "[condemn] most composers to seeking their livelihood elsewhere than in the writing of
music."

122. "Influence, Problem, Tone." *Dance Index,* 6 (1947): 249.
(Reprint—In *Stravinsky in the Theatre.* Edited by Minna Led-
erman, pp. 121–122. New York: Pellegrini & Cudahy, 1949.
Also Reprint—New York: Da Capo Press, 1975. 228 p. ISBN
0306706652. ML410 .S932L4 1975. Also Reprint in "The
Composer: Igor Stravinsky," in *Copland on Music.*)

In comparing Igor Stravinsky's influence to Richard Wagner's, Copland marvels at Stravinsky's ability to influence two succeeding

generations in diametrically opposed ways. The first generation of composers was influenced by his displaced accents and polytonal chords, the second generation by his neoclassicism. Copland predicts a third type of influence exploring issues of musical coherence, based on "formal-structural peculiarities" of works such as *Scènes de ballet, Ebony Concerto,* and *Symphony in Three Movements.* Even more impressive to Copland than Stravinsky's extended influence and ability to continue to create problematic music is his personal "tone," which defied description and imitation.

123. "International Music Congress—Forum." *Music & Artists,* 2 (February–March 1969): 23–29.

This is an edited transcription of a panel discussion, "The Sounds of Things to Come," which Copland moderated at the International Music Congress's 1968 meeting entitled "Music and Communication." Copland expresses concerns about the direction of contemporary music with its "almost *too* generous" attitude "toward all the many possibilities of music, including the latest instruments invented by scientists, [and] the possibilities opened up by the various mixed media." The panelists included Earl Brown (U.S.A.), Elliott Carter (U.S.A.), Peter Maxwell Davies (England), John Eaton (U.S.A.), Morton Feldman (U.S.A.), Gilles Lefebvre (Canada), Ben Johnston (U.S.A.), Pauline Oliveros (U.S.A.), Murray Schaefer (Canada), Roger Sessions (U.S.A.), Laszlo Somfai (Hungary), Morton Subotnick (U.S.A.), and Paul Williams (U.S.A.).

124. "Intro[duction] to Claire Reis'[s] book, *Composers, conductors and critics,* 1974." n.d. MS. 199/12, Aaron Copland Collection. Music Division, Library of Congress, Washington, DC.

See: Preface to *Composers, Conductors, and Critics,* by Claire R. Reis.

125. "Irving Fine." *Music of Irving Fine,* Boston Symphony Orchestra. RCA LSC 2829 (1966) [disc notes].

In these program notes Copland reviews Irving Fine's *Serious Song, Toccata,* and *Symphony,* as recorded by the Boston Symphony Orchestra. Copland's assessment of Fine's musicianship is virtually identical to "A Composer's Praise," but he adds commentary on the specific compositions. Copland laments that Fine would not be able to bring to fruition the new and "more adventurous" frame of reference expressed in his symphony. See: "Irving Fine (1914-1962)."

126. "Irving Fine (1914–1962)." 1962. MS. 199/13, Aaron Copland Collection. Music Division, Library of Congress, Washington, DC.

This is the typescript for "Irving Fine." See: "Irving Fine."

127. "Is the University Too Much with Us?" *New York Times*, 26 July 1970, sec. 2, pp. 13, 22.

The university campus has become a center of contemporary music-making in part because the institution can supply "the hall, the performers, and the audience and sometimes even a paying job for the composer." After recounting a brief history of musical radicalism on various university campuses over the previous two decades, Copland discusses the pros and cons of the university as patron, including the possible overemphasis of chamber music to the exclusion of orchestral genres, and the "ever present hazard of the academic environment" to focus on compositional analysis rather than musicality. Copland laments that few works have left the university environment to become staples of the concert repertoire, because new music "must invade our normal concert life." See: "Composers in the University."

128. "Is There a Revolution in the Arts?" *Town Meeting: Bulletin of America's Town Meeting of the Air*, 5 (19 February 1940): 17–20.

After probing the question of revolution in music, Copland discusses the changes brought to music by the electronic media—recordings, radio, and film. With the advent of a new mass audience, the composer no longer writes solely for the concert hall—a type of "musical museum." Copland states, "the spread of good music among millions of new listeners is certain to have as profound an effect on composers as the spread of literacy had upon writers. For the first time, democracy has entered the realm of music."

129. "The Ives Case."

See: "One Hundred and Fourteen Songs."

130. "Jak słuchać muzyki współczesnej" ("Listening to Contemporary Music"). *Ameryka*, 80 (n.d.): 8–9.

This article, published for distribution in Poland by the United States Information Agency, is a Polish translation of the chapter "Contemporary Music" from *What to Listen for in Music*. See: "A Modernist Defends Modern Music," "Contemporary Music—Is It Peculiar?" and "Contemporary Music" in *What to Listen for in Music*.

131. "Jazz   Structure   and   Influence."   *Modern   Music*,   4 (January–February 1927): 9-14.

In this article, Copland joins the debate on the definition of jazz. Arguing that its essence is formal, Copland advises that the first step toward understanding jazz is "a study of the mechanics of its frame." Copland provides various musical examples of the rhythmic development of jazz from ragtime, the fox-trot, and the Charleston, to alternating meters and polyrhythms. Although polyrhythms are not unique to jazz, the "peculiar excitement they produce by clashing two definitely and regularly marked rhythms is unprecedented in occidental music." Copland predicts that jazz will not become *passé* in the United States and that its polyrhythms will enrich all genres. See: "The Jazz Interlude" in *Our New Music* and *The New Music*.

132. "John Cage and the Music of Chance."

See: "The Music of Chance."

133. "Kann ein Komponist vom Komponieren leben?" *Melos*, 36 (April 1969): 156.

In this brief update, written in English and translated into German, Copland outlines the primary ways that an American composer can earn a living from composing—payments of performance rights, royalties from the sale and rental of published music, income from the sale of recordings, and commissions. Despite these venues, few art music composers earn a living solely from composition.

134. "Komponisten ohne Glorienschein." *Stimmen Monatsblätter fur Musik*, 1 (December 1947): 33.

According to Copland's handwritten note, this is a translation of "Composers without a Halo" from *Our New Music* and *The New Music*.

135. "The Late Romantics: Strauss, Mahler, Scriabin, Fauré, Sibelius."

See: "Five Post-Romantics."

136. "Latin Americans in Music." *WQXR Programs: June, 1942* (June 1942).

Following an extended tour of South America, Copland reported on the influence of indigenous and folk music on the art music of Latin America. He predicts that countries "with the richest folk material" would develop their art music most quickly, but that too much folk influence could make a country's art music provincial. In countries where the indigenous culture is separated from the dominant culture, "serious music is still closely allied in spirit to its European counterpart." Copland concludes that North and South America have faced Europe for "musical sustenance," but that now they should "turn about and face each other." Half of this brief article is an excerpt from "The Composers of South America: 1941" in *Copland on Music.*

137. "Leon Kirchner (1950)."

See: "Leon Kirchner: Duo for Violin and Piano."

138. "Leon Kirchner: Duo for Violin and Piano." *Music Library Association Notes*, 2d ser., 7 (June 1950): 434. (Reprint— "Leon Kirchner [1950]." In *Copland on Music.*)

Leon Kirchner's first published composition, Duo for Violin and Piano, creates a "strong impression" in live performance but contains little remarkable on the page in melodic invention, rhythmic novelty, or harmonic vocabulary. Copland cites Kirchner's "daringly free structural organization" as his "principal claim to originality." Live performances of Kirchner's works left the impression of "having made contact, not merely with a composer, but with a highly sentient human being; of a man who creates his music out of an awareness of the special climate of today's unsettled world."

139. "Letter on Gustav Mahler."

See: "[Letter to the Editor] Defends the Music of Mahler."

140. "Letters to Nicolas Slonimsky and to Arthur V. Berger." In *Letters of Composers: An Anthology*. Edited by Gertrude Norman and Miriam Lubell Shrifte, pp. 401–404. New York: Grosset & Dunlap, 1946. xviii, 422, xx p. ML90 .N67 1946.

In the letter to Nicolas Slonimsky (1927), Copland thanks him for sending reader responses written to various Boston newspapers following the premiere of the Piano Concerto. Copland reflects briefly on some of these responses. In his letter to Arthur Berger (1934), Copland responds to a request for some notes on his *Piano Variations*, tracing the compositional and performance history (mentioning Martha Graham) of the work. In a 1943 letter to Berger, Copland corrects various perceptions of his Piano Sonata, in response to Berger's publication in *Partisan Review*. Copland chides Berger for overdoing "the dichotomy between [Copland's] 'severe' and 'simple' styles."

141. "[Letter to the Editor] Defends the Music of Mahler." *New York Times*, 5 April 1925, sec. 9, p. 6.

While Copland agrees that New York City critics' reviews of Gustav Mahler as "bombastic, long-winded, [and] banal" were justified, he states that "it is what they leave unsaid that seems to me unfair." Copland viewed Mahler as "a composer of today" in his economic orchestration, polyphonic writing, and individual quality. Copland concludes that he could find no bombast in works such as *Das Lied von der Erde*.

142. "[Letter to Editor?] For the Record!" [1972]. MS. 199/2, Aaron Copland Collection. Music Division, Library of Congress, Washington, DC.

This is a typescript draft for "[Letters to the Editor] Varèse." In this draft Copland focuses on the importance of the League of Composers to the history of contemporary music in the United States from the 1920s to the 1940s. Of the 1,200 works performed by the League of Composers, 110 were commissioned and many others were American or world premieres. See: "[Letter to Editor], *New York Times,* 27 April 1972" and "[Letter to Editor] Varèse."

143. "[Letter to Editor] From the Mail Pouch: The Composers Ob[ject]: A Response from Eleven Who Were Represented at Critics' Concert." *New York Times,* 24 May 1942, sec. 8, p. 6.

In this letter to the music editor, Copland speaks for eleven composers (Arthur Berger, Edward T. Cone, Aaron Copland, Henry Cowell, David Diamond, Anis Fuleihan, Alexei Haieff, Frederick Jacobi, J. B. Middleton, Harold Morris, and William Schuman) in expressing offense at Olin Downes's criticism of two concerts of American music, presented by the Music Critics Circle. Although the works were selected by the critics themselves from premieres by prestigious ensembles, Downes did not "hesitate to lambast [*sic*] savagely and hold up to ridicule ten of the twelve works." Although recently elected chair of the Critics Circle, Downes claimed to have "'nothing to do with the selection' . . . and to disavow the considered judgment of certain of his colleagues." See: "[Letter to Editor re: Olin Downes]."

144. "[Letter to Editor], *New York Times,* n.d." MS. 199/22, Aaron Copland Collection. Music Division, Library of Congress, Washington, DC.

This is the handwritten draft of "[Letter to the Editor] *The Naked Image.*" See: "[Letter to the Editor] *The Naked Image.*"

145. "[Letter to Editor], *New York Times,* 27 April 1972." MS. 199/21, Aaron Copland Collection. Music Division, Library of Congress, Washington, DC.

This is a typescript for "[Letter to the Editor] Varèse." See: "[Letter to Editor?] For the Record!" and "[Letter to the Editor] Varèse."

146. "[Letter to Editor re: Olin Downes]." n.d. MS. 199/23, Aaron Copland Collection. Music Division, Library of Congress, Washington, DC.

This is a typescript draft of "From the Mail Pouch: The Composers Ob[ject]." See: "[Letter to Editor] From the Mail Pouch: The Composers Ob[ject]: A Response from Eleven Who Were Represented at Critics' Concert."

147. "[Letter to the Editor] *The Naked Image.*" *New York Times,* 4 September 1966, sec. 7, p. 18.

In this letter to the editor, Copland states that he had not sent a letter to the *New York Times* since 1925: "It's taken me 41 years to get sufficiently aroused to send a second letter, this time to protest the attempted down-grading of Harold Clurman in the review of his new book of drama criticism, *The Naked Image.*" An uncharacteristically agitated Copland writes: "Your reviewer . . . may be a big shot in the pages of the *Tulane Drama Review,* and he clearly considers himself a whiz at detecting outmoded ideas in the writings of others, but where in hell did he get the notion . . . that 'it's harder to write a good review than a good play'?" See: "[Letter to Editor], *New York Times.* n.d." MS. 199/22.

148. "[Letter to the Editor] Varèse." *New York Times,* 13 August 1972, sec. 7, p. 24.

According to Copland, Joan Peyser inserted "gratuitous musical politics" into her review of Louise Varèse's biography of her husband, Edgard Varèse. Louise Varèse relayed a "partisan account" of the split between Varèse's International Composers Guild and Claire Reis's League of Composers, with which Copland was affiliated. In an uncharacteristically agitated response to Peyser's statement that the League of Composers "promoted neo-classicism . . . at the expense of advanced composition," Copland responds that under the devoted leadership of Claire Reis, the League of Composers had propagated "works of living composers of every possible stripe and complexion." See: "[Letter to Editor?] For the Record!" and "[Letter to Editor], *New York Times,* 27 April 1972."

149. "[Letter to Music Editor] Letter from Composer." *New York Times,* 10 October 1954, sec. 2, p. 9.

In an editorial response to "Première in News," Copland expresses growing concern over the lack of composers in their twenties and thirties programmed on regular subscription concerts. The repertory of American works by mature composers is the result of conductors programming works by the same composers early in their career. "As cultural leaders of their communities," orchestral managements should promote young talent, otherwise "they will be impoverishing the symphonic repertory of the future." See: "[Letter to Music Editor]." *New York Times,* 4 October 1954.

150. "[Letter to Music Editor]." *New York Times,* 4 October 1954. MS. 199/24, Aaron Copland Collection. Music Division, Library of Congress, Washington, DC.

This is the draft of the letter to the editor that was published as "[Letter to Music Editor]: Letter from Composer." See: "[Letter to Music Editor] Letter from Composer."

151. "*The Life and Music of Béla Bartók,* by Halsey Stevens [Book Review]."

See "The Essence Remained."

152. "The Life of Music." *Christian Science Monitor,* 27 January 1976, p. 25.

In this five-paragraph excerpt from *Music and Imagination,* Copland considers the role of imagination for the creator and the listener. Creative listening is a talent that can be developed, given two requisites: "first, the ability to open oneself up to musical experience; and secondly, the ability to evaluate critically that experience."

153. "Listening to Polyphonic Music." In *The Music Lover's Handbook.* Edited by Elie Siegmeister, pp. 105–106. New York: W. Morrow, 1943. xiii, 817 p. ML55 .S6.

In this chapter, comprised of extracts from "Musical Texture" in *What to Listen for in Music,* Copland constructs an exercise to aid the listener in correctly listening to polyphonic music. Although polyphonic music places greater demands on the listener, repeated listenings "keep up your interest better" than homophonic music. See: "Musical Texture" in *What to Listen for in Music.*

154. "Liszt As Pioneer."

See: "Franz Liszt" and "A Tribute to Franz Liszt."

155. "The Live Composer." 1939. MS. 199/26, Aaron Copland Collection. Music Division, Library of Congress, Washington, DC.

Only the first and fifth pages of this five-page typescript remain. Copland begins the draft with the same opening and anecdote as "The Composer Speaks Out! Meet the Composer!" A complete version of "The Live Composer" would be more lengthy than "The Composer Speaks Out! Meet the Composer!" as it also includes descriptions of composers' remunerations. See: "The Composer Speaks Out! Meet the Composer!"

156. "London: 1931."

See: "European Festivals and Premieres: A Glance Backward" and "Contemporaries at Oxford: 1931."

157. "The Lyricism of Milhaud." *Modern Music*, 6 (January–February 1929): 14–19. (Reprint—In *Our New Music* and *The New Music*.)

Copland laments that the current American response to Darius Milhaud's music ran from "uninterested" to "openly antagonistic." According to Copland, "no other living composer is less well understood" than Milhaud, who "has proved himself the most important figure among the younger Frenchmen." Copland describes the lyricism, simplicity, and charm of Milhaud's compositions and how the composer perpetuated his image as a musical antagonist. Copland chides people for their "illusion" that they knew Milhaud, based on only single hearings of several compositions.

158. "Making Music in the Star-Spangled Manner." *Music and Musicians*, 8 (August 1960): 8–9.

This article is the transcription of a talk on American music that Copland gave to London audiences. In the talk, he discusses the growing stature of American art music and the reasons—mainly a "primitive" musical superstructure and overreliance on European models—for its lack of musical exports until after World War I. Copland discusses the roots of the 1920s musical movement to create a recognizably American music through the use of jazz rhythms. Finally, he illustrates the differences between American and European rhythmic sense. See: "Search for an 'American' Music" and "A Businessman Who Wrote Music on Sundays."

159. "Marc Blitzstein." In *The Music Lover's Handbook.* Edited by Elie Siegmeister, pp. 761–764. New York: W. Morrow, 1943. xiii, 817 p. ML55 .S6.

This article is extracted from the chapter "Thomson and Blitzstein" in *Our New Music.* Copland evaluates Marc Blitzstein's stage works, a genre closer to musical theater than opera, in which Blitzstein capitalized on the naturalness of the singing actor. Blitzstein was the first American to apply the formula of "a cross between social drama, musical revue, and opera" in *The Cradle Will Rock.* In *No for an Answer,* "for the first time in a serious stage work [Blitzstein] gave the typical American tough guy musical characterization." See: "Thomson and Blitzstein" in *Our New Music* and *The New Music.*

160. "The Measure of Kapell." *Saturday Review,* 28 November 1953, p. 67. (Reprint—"The Pianist: William Kapell." In *Copland on Music.*)

In a letter written to William Kapell's widow after his death in October 1953, Copland proclaims Kapell "among the few top pianists of our time." Kapell was "profoundly the artist, both in his very nature and in the symbolic role he was fated to play in the concert world": "His programming was an act of faith; it was Willie's contribution toward a solution of one of the most disturbing factors in our musical life: namely, the loss of connection between the performer and the contemporary composer of his time." Kapell greatly admired Copland's works, repeatedly programming the most difficult of Copland's piano compositions in a "spirit of defiance."

161. ["Mellers, Wilfred Howard"]. 1965. MS. 199/29, Aaron Copland Collection. Music Division, Library of Congress, Washington, DC.

See: *Music in a New Found Land,* by Wilfred Howard Mellers [Book Review].

162. "Melody." In *What to Listen for in Music.* (Reprint—In *The New Music Lover's Handbook.* Edited by Elie Siegmeister,

pp. 54–56. Irvington-on-Hudson, NY: Harvey House, 1973.
620 p. ISBN 0817851518. ML55 .S62.)

In the musical fabric, melody is of secondary importance only to
rhythm. Copland identifies the elements of melodic construction—
diatonic and chromatic scale, mode, modulation, and tonic and
dominant tones—using these concepts to analyze melodic excerpts
from works of Giovanni Palestrina, J. S. Bach, Franz Schubert, Carlos Chávez, Roy Harris, and Arnold Schoenberg. After considering
the qualities of a beautiful melody, Copland cautions "Whatever
the quality of the melodic line considered alone, the listener must
never lose sight of its function in a composition. It should be followed like a continuous thread which leads the listener through a
piece from the very beginning to the very end."

163. "Memorial to Paul Rosenfeld." *Music Library Association
   Notes,* 2d ser., 4 (March 1947): 147–148. (Reprint without
   bibliography—"A Verdict." In *Paul Rosenfeld, Voyager in
   the Arts.* Edited by Jerome Mellquist and Lucie Wiese,
   pp. 166–169. New York: Creative Age Press, 1948 and 1954.
   Reprint. New York: Octagon Books, 1977. xxxv, 284 p. ISBN
   0374955611. ML55 .R65M4 1977. Also Reprint without
   bibliography—"The Critic: Paul Rosenfeld." In *Copland on
   Music.*)

Paul Rosenfeld was a composer's critic, proving that composer and
critic are not necessarily incompatible. A music lover first and a
critic second, Rosenfeld was as deeply involved in the musical culture as the composer. A champion of contemporary music, he was
the first to write seriously about Igor Stravinsky, Ernest Bloch,
Roger Sessions, Roy Harris, Carlos Chávez, Charles Ives, and
Edgard Varèse, among others. Rosenfeld identified a patron for the
young Copland, demonstrating that as a critic, Rosenfeld's support
for the composer extended beyond positive reviews.

164. "Mexican Composer." *New York Times,* 9 May 1937, sec.
   11, p. 5.

The recent musical movement in Mexico, comparable to the movement in Mexican painting led by Diego Rivera and José Orozco,
was the result of the efforts of composers Carlos Chávez and
Sylvestre Revueltas. More than Chávez, Revueltas "draws . . .

directly on actual tunes that originated from popular Mexican music, and he composes organically tunes which are almost indistinguishable from the original folk material." As an example of Revueltas's "extraordinary musicality and naturalness," Copland cites his "spontaneous outpouring, a strong expression of his inner emotions." Copland discusses Revueltas's Mexican nationalism in his concert music and in his film score for *Redes*.

165. "Miklós Rósza and Bernard Herrmann." n.d. MS. 199/30, Aaron Copland Collection. Music Division, Library of Congress, Washington, DC.

In this two-paragraph handwritten draft, Copland discusses the contributions of Bernard Herrmann and Miklós Rósza to the genre of film music. Herrmann, "one of the few men who has been able to introduce a few new ideas in the Hollywood musical scene," was especially notable for his innovative orchestrations (such as the use of eight celestas for sleigh ride music in *The Magnificent Ambersons*). Rósza, while not as experimental as Herrmann, wrote "in an idiom which takes full advantage of modern musical resources."

166. "Milhaud: First Symphony and *In Memoriam* (Columbia Album) and *Protée—Symphonic Suite No. 2* (Victor Album DM 1027)." n.d. MS. 199/31, Aaron Copland Collection. Music Division, Library of Congress, Washington, DC.

This is the typescript draft for "The Art of Darius Milhaud." See: "The Art of Darius Milhaud."

167. "Miscellany: Notes for Articles." n.d. MS. 202/24, Aaron Copland Collection. Music Division, Library of Congress, Washington, DC.

This is a handwritten and typed collection of notes and quotations on composers: J. S. Bach ("America should love Bach—He is the greatest of them all"), Ludwig van Beethoven ("Never understood how Beethoven was 'sold' to the big public"), Henry Purcell, Domenico Scarlatti, and Giuseppe Verdi ("Verdi is an object lesson to the intellectuals—Like [George] Gershwin—the faults are obvious—but they do not in the end influence the directness of appeal"). Among the notes Copland transcribed the following quotation: "At least, it is better to be spurred to acquire scholarship because you enjoy the poetry, than to suppose that you enjoy the poetry because you have acquired the scholarship. T. S. Eliot—Dante."

168. "Modern Music: 'Fresh and Different.'" *New York Times Magazine,* 13 March 1955, pp. 15, 60, 62. (Reprint—"'Are My Ears on Wrong?': A Polemic." In *Copland on Music.* Also Reprint—"Modern Music: 'Fresh and Different.'" In *The Meaning in Reading.* Edited by Jacob Hooper Wise, J. E. Congleton, and Alton C. Morris. 4th ed., pp. 243–245. New York: Harcourt, Brace, 1956. 265 p. PR1363 .W55 1956. Also Reprint—"Are My Ears on Wrong?" *San Francisco Symphony Program Notes,* February 1967, 6–7.)

Copland's "first and only essay in musical polemics," written for the *New York Times Magazine,* was a response to Henry Pleasants's book *The Agony of Modern Music* (1955). Pleasants theorized that classical music was "bankrupt" and "obsolete," and that the only true modern music was jazz, as indicated by the popular, commercial voice. Copland, arguing for the contemporary composer, specifies advancements made to the nineteenth-century vocabulary in specific musical elements. He illustrates that, while the audience for contemporary music is specialized, it is no less enthusiastic than the general audience. Copland critiques the use of conservative, profit-oriented programming policies to judge viability of contemporary music. He also argues the differences between popular (read "jazz") and art music.

169. "Modern Orchestration Surveyed." *Modern Music,* 8 (November–December 1930): 41–44.

Copland proclaims *Die Neue Instrumentation,* by Egon Wellesz, "a disappointing book but at least it makes a start in a much-neglected field." The main failing of the book was that, rather than focusing on the highlights of modern orchestration, Wellesz "tried to survey the entire field of orchestral literature with the inevitable result of obtaining only a very sketchy bird's eye view of the whole subject." Copland also critiques Wellesz's evaluation of the "five most important orchestrators of the twentieth century"—Gustav Mahler, Richard Strauss, Claude Debussy, Arnold Schoenberg, and Igor Stravinsky.

170. "The Modern Symphony." In *The Music Lover's Handbook.* Edited by Elie Siegmeister, pp. 125–126. New York: W. Morrow, 1943. xiii, 817 p. ML55 .S6.

In this article, abridged from the chapter "Sonata Form" in *What to Listen for in Music,* Copland briefly lists the composers currently writing in a symphonic form. After a short assessment of Gustav Mahler's and Jean Sibelius's contributions to the symphony, Copland concludes that the genre "is still as firmly established as ever." See: "Fundamental Form—IV. Sonata Form" in *What to Listen for in Music.*

171. "A Modernist Defends Modern Music." *New York Times Magazine,* 25 December 1949, pp. 11, 30–31. (Reprint— *Boston Symphony Orchestra Bulletin,* 14 [3 February 1950]: 760–773. Also Reprint in part—In *An Introduction to Music Publishing.* Edited by Carolyn Sachs. New York: C. F. Peters, 1981. 20 p. ISBN 0938856006. ML112 I58. Also Reprint in part—"Contemporary Music." In *What to Listen for in Music.*)

After fifty years, "modern music" still sounded peculiar to the general listener. Arguing that not all contemporary music is equally inaccessible, Copland constructs a list of current composers by levels of listening difficulty. He also addresses the most commonly asked questions about dissonance, melody, aloofness, and intellectual challenge in contemporary music. Copland concludes that contemporary music will remain "peculiar" to a listener "only so long as he persists in trying to hear the same kinds of sounds or derive the same species of musical pleasure that he gets from the great works of the past." This article is the basis for the chapter "Contemporary Music" in *What to Listen for in Music.* See: "Contemporary Music—Is It Peculiar?," "Jak słuchać muzyki współczesnej," and "Contemporary Music" in *What to Listen for in Music.*

172. "More Comments on Copland." *American Record Guide,* 44 (November 1980): 10–11.

In these comments, taken from CBS Records M2 35901, Copland discusses the role of the piano and creative inspiration in the compositional process. He also comments on the composer's confrontation with abstract formal structure and the experience of critiquing his music from the audience.

173. "Music and the Human Spirit."

See: "Music: As an Aspect of the Human Spirit" and "La música como aspecto del espiritu humano."

174. "Music and the Movies." 1949. n.d. MS. 200/1, Aaron Copland Collection. Music Division, Library of Congress, Washington, DC.

This is the typescript for "Tip to Moviegoers: Take Off Those Ear-Muffs." See: "Tip to Moviegoers: Take Off Those Ear-Muffs."

175. "Music: As an Aspect of the Human Spirit." In *Man's Right to Knowledge: An International Symposium Presented in Honor of the Two-Hundredth Anniversary of Columbia University, 1754–1954.* 2d Series: Present Knowledge and New Directions, pp. 99–106. New York: Herbert Muschel, 1954. (Reprint—"Music and the Human Spirit." *Musical Courier,* 151 [1 February 1955]: 54–56. Also Reprint—"Music As an Aspect of the Human Spirit." In *Copland in Music.*)

As part of Columbia University's bicentennial celebration, Copland was asked to speak on "Music As an Aspect of the Human Spirit." He expounded on the daily act of composing as "the expression by way of music of a basic need of the human spirit." Although the meaning of music is too "amorphous and intangible" to put into words, "the art of music demonstrates a man's ability to transmute the substance of his everyday experience into a body of sound that has coherence and direction and flow, unfolding its own life in a meaningful and natural way in time and in space." Music is differentiated from all the other arts in its melding of emotional and conscious understanding—"musical cerebration directed towards an emotionally purposeful end." Copland also reflected on radical musical change in the past, present, and future of Western art music. See: "La música como aspecto del espiritu humano."

176. "*Music for the Theatre.*" n.d. MS. 200/2, Aaron Copland Collection. Music Division, Library of Congress, Washington, DC.

This is the typescript for "Some Notes on My *Music for the The-atre.*" See: "Some Notes on My *Music for the Theatre.*"

177. "Music in America: Past, Present, and Future." n.d. MS. 200/3, Aaron Copland Collection. Music Division, Library of Congress, Washington, DC.

Copland disputes the opinion held by "many well-meaning Euro-peans" that "the commercial prowess of the American precludes the possibility of his possessing any artistic talents whatsoever." He argues that in the United States, a relative absence of war and poverty allowed a "kind of spiritual energy" to be expressed in the arts. Development of American music, whether past, present, or fu-ture, depends on a superstructure comprised of three factors: "a creative school of native composers, a full flowering of interpretive artists and organizations, and a country-wide body of intelligent lis-teners."

178. *Music in a New Found Land,* by Wilfred Howard Mellers [Book Review]. *The Borzoi Quarterly,* 14 (Second Quarter 1965): 4.

This is a single-paragraph review of *Music in a New Found Land,* by Wilfrid Howard Mellers. Copland describes the book as "unique": "For the first time the whole panorama of contemporary American composition has been brought into focus by a perceptive and qualified writer-musician, and an Englishman at that." Al-though Copland had reservations about some of Mellers's judg-ments and decisions, he felt the book was an important documentation of the development of twentieth-century American culture through music. See: ["Mellers, Wilfred Howard"].

179. "Music in Cuba." 1941. MS. 200/4, Aaron Copland Collec-tion. Music Division, Library of Congress, Washington, DC.

This unpublished typescript, a report detailing the lack of musical superstructure in Cuba, was written for the Music Committee of the Coordinator's Office. Lacking his characteristic optimism about Latin American music, Copland reports on the death of Cuba's two most prominent classical composers, discusses the primarily social function of the Orquesta Filharmonic de la Habana, and notes the general absence of music conservatories, radio broadcasts of classical music, and publication opportunities for Cuban composers. Although popular music was Cuba's strongest musical asset, no book had been written on the subject.

180. "Music in the Air." n.d. MS. 200/5, Aaron Copland Collection. Music Division, Library of Congress, Washington, DC.

In this review of current radio broadcasts, Copland lists all of the weekend classical music programs ("a clear case of week-end musical indigestion"), critiquing the repertory as primarily "a limited supply of famous musical chestnuts," that neglected contemporary American music. Noting the change to vinyl in the recording industry, Copland reviews recorded performances of primarily nineteenth-century standard compositions, in addition to performances of popular songs such as "Stardust," "Grandfather's Clock," and "That for Me" (from *State Fair*).

181. "Music in the Films."

See: "Second Thoughts on Hollywood."

182. "Music Is the Message." *Christian Science Monitor,* 22 July 1976, p. 24.

In this two-paragraph excerpt from *Music and Imagination,* Copland concludes that the meaning of music is "many-sided and can be approached from many different angles." He unites aestheticians' opposing theories that music has no extramusical connotation and that music is a symbolic language to be interpreted subjectively.

183. "Music: My Way of Life." *Boys' Life,* 54 (December 1964): 28, 67–68.

Answering the question "Should you be a composer?" for the *Boys' Life* audience, Copland concludes that if you must compose, you will. To help the audience understand what is involved in a life of musical composition, Copland recounts his own compositional education, theorizes about what an artist attempts to accomplish, and explains the importance of being "part of the American scene in music." Stating that although "composing is my life, it doesn't

mean that nothing else is important," Copland discusses the importance of writing, teaching, and "music citizenship."

184. "The Music of Chance." In *The New Music*. (Reprint—"John
Cage and the Music of Chance." In *The New Music Lover's
Handbook*. Edited by Elie Siegmeister, pp. 542–544. Irving-
on-Hudson, NY: Harvey House, 1973. 620 p. ISBN
0817851518. ML55 .S62.)

Copland recounts a brief history of John Cage as the "inventor of
chance music" and the prepared piano. Copland then surveys the
"different versions of the principle of indeterminacy" as expressed
by Karlheinz Stockhausen, Pierre Boulez, Henry Brant, Morton
Feldman, Lukas Foss, and Earle Brown. Among the results of
chance music have been the exploration of new performance techniques and invention of new notations. Copland's bias against the
music of chance is summed up in his conclusion: "The process is
amusing to contemplate; but the question remains of whether it can
hold the continuing interest of a rational mind."

185. "*The Music of Israel,* by Peter Gradenwitz, New York: W. W.
Norton, Inc. Reviewed by Aaron Copland." n.d. MS. 200/6,
Aaron Copland Collection. Music Division, Library of Con-
gress, Washington, DC.

See: "What Is Jewish Music?"

186. "Music Out of Everywhere." Review of *Notes without Music:
An Autobiography,* by Darius Milhaud. *New York Times,* 22
February 1953, sec. 7, p. 7.

Copland's review of Darius Milhaud's autobiography, *Notes without Music,* is as much a statement of what Copland admired about
Milhaud and his music as a book review. Always a champion of
Milhaud's music in the United States, Copland states that the autobiography is "an engaging self-portrait by Darius Milhaud, one of
the world's most gifted composers." As the title suggests, Milhaud
found pretexts for "making music everywhere," in a celebration of
"his family, social or religious life." In *Notes without Music,* Milhaud's literary style mirrored his musical aesthetic in its "relaxed
and natural manner." See: "*Notes without Music.* By Darius Milhaud." [Book Review].

187. "Music Since 1920." *Modern Music*, 5 (March–April 1928): 16–20.

Copland's overview of aesthetics of the 1920s was written as an attempt "to clarify the present status of new music." He describes the years 1920 to 1928 as "a period of repose in which the full energy of the composer [was] directed toward the creation of perfected masterworks." While the 1920s were not characterized by the same radical experimentation seen in the first decades of the twentieth century, 1920 did mark a new interest in aesthetic theories and structural problems.

188. "La música como aspecto del espiritu humano." *Nuestro Tiempo*, 3, no. 14 (n.d.).

According to Copland's notation, this is a translation of "Music: As an Aspect of the Human Spirit." (The citation on Copland's offprint of the article does not match the bound journals.) See: "Music: As an Aspect of the Human Spirit."

189. "La música en el extranjero." *Musicalia*, 4 (May–June 1941): 29–31.

Copland reviews the eighteenth Festival of the International Society of Contemporary Music for the Spanish reader, as a type of public relations, since the next festival could be held in a Latin American country. Copland discusses compositions by William Alwyn, Henk Badings, Benjamin Britten, Willy Burkhard, Copland, Paul Dessau, Jerzy Fitelberg, Rodolfo Halffter, Piet Ketting, René Leibowitz, Bohuslav Martinů, Charles Naginski, Roman Palester, Mátyás Seiber, Viktor Szalowski, and Bernard Wagenaar.

190. "La musica moderna è nata in reazione a Wagner." *L'avienire d'Italia*, 56 (16 May 1951). (Also—"Musica moderna e musica romantica." *Pomeriggio*, 18 May 1951.)

This brief article, in addition to a short introduction to Copland himself, covers the birth of modern music (Claude Debussy, Modest Mussorgsky, and Mikhail Glinka) in reaction to romantic composers such as Richard Wagner.

191. "La musica per film: nuovo mezzo di espressione musicale." *Il mattino d'Italia*, 9 March (n.d.).

According to Copland's notation, this is a translation of "Tip to Moviegoers: Take Off Those Ear-Muffs." See: "Tip to Moviegoers: Take Off Those Ear-Muffs."

192. "The Musical Scene Changes." *Twice a Year,* 5–6 (Fall–Winter 1940, Spring–Summer 1941): 340–343.

In its understated way, this is virtually a manifesto of Copland's beliefs over the first decades of his compositional career. The "period of experimental change in music . . . was an attempt to free music from the conventions—rhythmical, harmonic, formal—that had gradually been stifling all freshness." The period of specialized concerts and audiences (1920–1930), gave way to a need to communicate to the larger audiences made available through recordings, radio, and film. (Among the first leaders in this wider accessibility were Paul Hindemith, Kurt Weill, Ernst Krenek, and Dmitri Shostakovich.) The composer "must embody new communal ideals in a new communal music." See: "The Present Day" in *Our New Music.*

193. "Musical Texture."

See: "Listening to Polyphonic Music."

194. "Musikalisches Schaffen in Amerika." *Österreichische Musikzeitschrift,* 20 (May–June 1965): 266–270.

This article is a translated excerpt from "Creativity in America" from *Copland on Music.* See: "Creativity in America."

195. "Nadia Boulanger." *Pauta,* 5 (1986): 20–25.

This is a Spanish translation of "Nadia Boulanger, Mother of Modern Music." See: "Nadia Boulanger, Mother of Modern Music."

196. "Nadia Boulanger: An Affectionate Portrait." *Harper's,* 221 (October 1960): 49–51. (Reprint—"The Teacher: Nadia Boulanger." In *Copland on Music.*)

Despite biographical information on Copland, Nadia Boulanger, and their relationship, the purpose of the article is "to concentrate on her principal attribute, her gift as teacher." The article includes an updated discussion of women composition teachers and composers. Yet rather than considering Boulanger a composer, Copland places her in the lineage of the French intellectual woman with a salon. Among Boulanger's strongest gifts as a teacher were her intellectual interests in all the arts, knowing "everything there was to know about music," her perceptivity as a musician, and her ability to inspire self-confidence in a young composer. Copland concludes that "America, unfortunately, has no reward commensurate with what Boulanger has contributed to our musical development." See: "Nadya Bulanzhe—Uchitel' kompozitsii" and "The Teacher: Nadia Boulanger."

197. "Nadia Boulanger, Mother of Modern Music." 1981. MS. 200/14, Aaron Copland Collection. Music Division, Library of Congress, Washington, DC.

Copland wrote this tribute following Boulanger's death in 1979. In it he does not attempt to be analytical, but is highly anecdotal, narrative, and personal. Included in the typescript draft are scenes from Boulanger's last years, in addition to often-repeated descriptions of their first encounter and her teaching studio. Some of these references are more complete than in other published versions. See: "Nadia Boulanger."

198. "Nadya Bulanzhe—Uchitel' kompozitsii." *Sovetskaia muzyka,* 28 (June 1964): 120-122.

This is an excerpt from *Copland on Music* on Nadia Boulanger. The citation is unverified. See: "Nadia Boulanger: An Affectionate Portrait."

199. "Neglected Works: A Symposium." *Modern Music,* 23 (Winter 1946): 3–12.

Copland lists by genre neglected works from the modern repertory. He states, "I get a kind of nausea when I think of the waste all the unplayed music represents." Among the neglected works are compositions by Marc Blitzstein, Carlos Chávez, Manuel de Falla, Charles Ives, Darius Milhaud, Robert Palmer, Erik Satie, Roger Sessions, Edgard Varèse, and Stefan Wolpe ("the most unjustly neglected composer in America today").

200. "Eine neue amerikanische Komponistengeneration." *Neue Auslese,* 3 (June 1948): 69–73.

This article is a translation of "The New 'School' of American Composers." See: "The New 'School' of American Composers" and "Nueva generatión de compositores norteaméricanos."

201. "New Books: Thomson's Musical State."

See: "Thomson's Musical State."

202. "New Electronic Media." In *The New Music.* (Reprint—In *The New Music Lover's Handbook.* Edited by Elie Siegmeister, pp. 430–433. Irvington-on-Hudson, NY: Harvey House, 1973. 620 p. ISBN 0817851518. ML55 .S62.)

"With the introduction of electronic music . . . science and scientific calculation were injected into our musical thinking." Although diplomatically listing advantages (help in copying scores and parts, increased musical dissemination, and novelty) as well as disadvantages (elimination of live performers and "depressing sameness of sound") of the electronic media, and allowing the new generation of composers the "benefit of the doubt," Copland was clearly disturbed by the new developments. He feared that the field of composition was "being taken over by the engineers and technicians," placing composers "in danger of being put out of their own house." He states: "Just as the world at large has the problem of how to absorb and incorporate the phenomenal advances of the scientific age without loss of our humanity, so the musical world must face a similar solution." After tracing by decade the "gradual infiltration of scientific ideas" in recent music, Copland concludes: "With open minds and a good amount of forbearance the musical challenges of the future will have to be met."

203. "New Music in the U.S.A."

See: "The Composer in America, 1923–1933."

204. "New Records." *Modern Music,* 16 (March–April 1939): 185–188.

Copland reviews record releases by Roy Harris (Chorale for string sextet), Deems Taylor (suite from *Alice in Wonderland*), Paul Hindemith (String Quartet No. 3), and Dmitri Shostakovich (excerpts from *The Age of Gold*). He also reviews vernacular and popular music releases: a recording of the Old Harp Singers of Nashville,

Tennessee; the first releases by Blue Note Records; and music from Tahiti, Peru, and the Belgian Congo.

205. "The New 'School' of American Composers." *New York Times Magazine,* 14 March 1948, pp. 18, 51–54. (Reprint—"1949: The New 'School' of American Composers." In *Copland on Music.*)

"You cannot set up a continuing tradition of creative music in any country without a constant freshening of source material as each decade brings forth a new batch of composers." Yet this younger generation must be nurtured, assuring them "sound musical training, that their first successful efforts are heard, and that they feel themselves part of the musical movement of their country." Copland characterizes the generation of composers, then approximately thirty years old, as possessing "a wide variety of compositional interests rather than any one unified tendency." These composers generally have not been to Europe, but have been influenced by Europeans in the United States and the previous generations of American composers. Included are the following seven composers: Leonard Bernstein ("At its best, his is music of vibrant rhythmic invention, irresistible elan, terrific punch"), Harold Shapero ("Gifted and baffling; his adroitness is placed at the service of a wonderful musical gift"), Alexei Haieff ("Sensitive and refined; his pieces have personality, sensibility and wit; they divert and delight"), Robert Palmer ("Always his music has urgency; it seems to come from some inner need for expression"), John Cage ("One of the curiosities of the younger generation; his music stems from Balinese and Hindu styles"), Lukas Foss ("The *Wunderkind* of this group; his music has spontaneity and naturalness, absolute clarity of texture"), and William Bergsma ("A sober and serious workman with a poetic and critical mind; one of the solid values of today's music"). Copland concludes, "If we can gauge the musical future of a nation by the healthy activity of its younger generation of composers, then America is likely to do well." See: "Eine neue amerikanische Komponistengeneration," "Nueva generatión de compositores norteaméricanos," and "The Youngest Generation of American Composers."

206. "Night Thoughts." In *A Garland for Charles Ives: Parnassus: Poetry in Review,* Spring/Summer 1975, p. 295–299.

This special supplement to *Parnassus* includes a copy of Copland's piano composition "Night Thoughts," subtitled "Homage to Ives."

207. "1949: The New 'School' of American Composers."

See: "The New 'School' of American Composers."

208. "1936: America's Young Men—Ten Years Later."

See: "Our Younger Generation Ten Years Later."

209. "1926: America's Young Men of Promise."

See: "America's Young Men of Promise."

210. "None in the Same Way." *Christian Science Monitor,* 19 September 1979, p. 21.

In this two-paragraph excerpt from *Music and Imagination,* Copland answers the questions Why must a composer create? and Why is that creative impulse never satisfied? He writes: "I must create in order to know myself, and since self-knowledge is a never-ending search, each new work is only a part-answer to the question 'Who am I?.'"

211. "A Note on Irving Fine," 1962. MS. 200/17, Aaron Copland Collection. Music Division, Library of Congress, Washington, DC.

This is the typescript for "A Composer's Praise." See: "A Composer's Praise."

212. "A Note on Nadia Boulanger." *The Fontainebleau Alumni Bulletin,* 5 (May 1930): 1.

Copland wrote this article on Nadia Boulanger for the tenth anniversary of the Fontainebleau School of Music. One trait that was "most remarkable in this most remarkable woman" was her love of music—"a selfless and consuming passion [implying] a purity of spirit combined with a youthful, eager and naive quality that few possess." Her love of music added extra significance to her technical mastery of music, making her "alive to the music of [the] day" and a successful teacher. Rather than a superficial or faddish support of the American composer's "expression of national consciousness," she sought "the profound personality as beyond a question of territorial boundaries."

213. "A Note on Young Composers." *Music Vanguard: A Critical Review,* 1 (March–April 1935): 14–16.

Unlike when Copland returned from his studies in Paris during the 1920s, the young composer in the mid-1930s was faced with relatively more complex issues—scarcity of money and no singular society for the presentation of modern music. Those who followed the models of Arnold Schoenberg or Igor Stravinsky have realized that such older styles do not speak to contemporary audiences, and have thrown "in their lot with that of the working class." New problems have arisen with this new audience: "the style and content of their music, practical possibilities (usually limitations) in performance, sectarian dangers, etc., which do not obtain in the same way in the ordinary bourgeois field of music." Young composers who ally themselves with "the proletarian movement" must realize "what such a step means, if [their] work is to be of permanent value to the workers and their cause." In retrospect it is easy to see how such sentiments led to accusations of Copland's Communist sympathies, even though they are clearly an expression of the time.

214. "Notes on a Cowboy Ballet." [1938]. MS. 200/19, Aaron Copland Collection. Music Division, Library of Congress, Washington, DC.

In this four-page typescript, Copland tells of the origins and scenario of *Billy the Kid.* In hindsight the use of cowboy tunes in the ballet seems inevitable, so it is interesting to read of Copland's initial distaste for the musical material of the tunes: "As far as I was concerned, this ballet could be written without benefit of the poverty-stricken tunes Billy himself must have known." As in other sources, Copland discusses the difficulty of adding harmonic accompaniment to well-known melodies and the requisite simplicity needed for Billy the Kid's character.

215. "*Notes without Music,* by Darius Milhaud." [Book Review]. 1953. MS. 200/20, Aaron Copland Collection. Music Division, Library of Congress, Washington, DC.

This is the typescript for "Music Out of Everywhere." See: "Music Out of Everywhere."

216. "Nueva generatión de compositores norteaméricanos." *Nuestra musica: Revista trimestral editada en Mexico,* 2 (July 1947): 129–137.

This article is a translation of "The New 'School' of American Composers." See: "The New 'School' of American Composers" and "Eine neue amerikanische Komponistengeneration."

217. "On Being a Composer." n.d. MS. 200/22, Aaron Copland Collection. Music Division, Library of Congress, Washington, DC.

This handwritten outline is titled variously "Composer Shop-Talk: On Being a Composer—The Composer's Primer—Composers' Handbook." Copland included the following topics for consideration: (1) How You Get That Way/Creativity—What It Is, (2) The Composers [*sic*] Life, (3) The Composers [*sic*] Job, (4) Interpret [*sic*], (5) Public, (6) Admirers and Wives, (7) Economics, (8) Composer & the Past, (9) Composer & the Future, and (10) Critics.

218. "On Music Composition." In *The Creative Mind and Method: Exploring the Nature of Creativeness in American Arts, Sciences, and Professions.* Edited by Jack D. Summerfield and Lorlyn Thatcher, pp. 29–33. New York: Russell & Russell, 1964, [c. 1960]. xvi, 118 p. BF408 .S85 1964.

In this article, Copland discusses compositional process in collaborative and functional musics, equating the compositional process in choreographic and film music. He argues that music written for other than the concert hall is not, "by definition, more minor." Among the reasons to compose functional music, Copland numbers financial benefits, the ability to reach a wide audience, and a talent for that arena. Copland ties the interest in using folk material to express an American voice to the building of folk music archives by the Library of Congress.

219. "On the Notation of Rhythm." *Modern Music,* 21 (May–June 1944): 217–220. (Reprint—"Shop Talk: On the Notation of Rhythm." In *Copland on Music.*)

This article illustrates Copland's involvement with theoretical issues of contemporary music, such as the notation of technically problematic "modern rhythms." At issue is whether or not "'meter and rhythm are synonymous.'" Copland debates the subtleties between notating an asymmetrical pattern of two and three eighth notes as a constant meter with shifting accents or as shifting meters with constant accents on the downbeat of each measure. Although Copland concludes that composers should "notate their music so that, as far as possible, it looks the way it sounds," he concedes that variables such as instrumentation, length of the asymmetrical patterns, and whether or not the barline is an indication of rhythmic stress make it impossible to generalize for every case.

220. "On the Occasion of the 70th Birthday of Serge Prokofieff." 1961. MS. 200/24, Aaron Copland Collection. Music Division, Library of Congress, Washington, DC.

This typescript was written for *Sovetskaia muzyka* to commemorate the seventieth birthday of Sergei Prokofiev. Copland describes his introduction to Prokofiev during a meeting with Sergey Koussevitzky at the conductor's house, where Copland had gone to play a new composition. Prokofiev responded to Copland's composition with a blunt honesty, typical of his personality and music. Prokofiev's music never ceases to astonish Americans with the "richness of its invention: the never-ending welling up of fresh melodies, the charm or bite of the harmonies, the bounce and dash of the rhythms. To us, [Prokofiev] is a profoundly national composer who knew how to speak in a universal tongue."

221. "One Hundred and Fourteen Songs." *Modern Music,* 11 (January–February 1934): 59–64.

Copland's own concerns over an audience for contemporary music influenced his overall assessment of Charles Ives's compositions and writings from *114 Songs.* Copland surveys and categorizes the collection of songs, concluding that they were "unique and memorable . . . ; a contribution which, for richness and depth of emotional content, for broad range and strength of expression, for harmonic and rhythmic originality, will remain a challenge and an inspiration to future generations of American composers." Copland judges the weaknesses of Ives's compositional style to be the result of an isolation from an audience—"a lack of that kind of self-criticism which only actual performance and public reaction can bring"—and concludes that an audience must be found for composers such as Ives, "or American music will never be born." See: "The Ives Case" in *Our New Music* and *The New Music*.

222. "An Open Letter about the BBC from Aaron Copland." BBC Symphony Orchestra Tour Brochure, 1965. [n.p.]

Copland wrote this letter of welcome and commendation for the British Broadcasting Corporation (BBC) Symphony Orchestra's first tour of the United States. Copland became associated with the BBC during trips to London in which he collaborated in various types of programs, including the Third Program, Invitations Concerts, sponsorship of regional orchestras, Talks Programs, and television documentaries (including "Mr. Copland Comes to Town"). The policies of the BBC, under the leadership of William Glock, have "furthered the cause of contemporary music everywhere."

223. "Oper für Amerika." In *Musik der Zeit: Lebt die Oper,* Neue Folge, Heft 3 (Bonn: Boosey & Hawkes, 1960), p. 26.

This article is a German translation of the typescript "Opera for America." See: "Opera for America."

224. "Opera for America (Written for *Musik der Zeit,* Bonn)." 1959. MS. 201/3, Aaron Copland Collection. Music Division, Library of Congress, Washington, DC.

The Ford Foundation had recently created a $950,000 grant to finance sixteen new American operas—an indication of the general excitement surrounding professional opera in the United States. American opera, however, is also characterized by community operas for which Copland wrote *The Tender Land.* Sensing a lack of repertory for young American singers, Copland wanted to create a work that spoke to the performers as Americans, with "a rhythm and melodic contour that reflects the characteristic inflection of American speech." Copland hoped that European productions of *The Tender Land* would prove that while its "treatment is American, . . . the theme is universal." See: "Oper für Amerika."

225. "Orchestral Magic." *Christian Science Monitor,* 30 January 1980, p. 20.

In this two-paragraph excerpt from *Music and Imagination,* Copland discusses Hector Berlioz as the inventor of the modern orchestra. Berlioz's "orchestral magic" came from his ability to blend instruments to achieve new results, to exploit particular registers of individual instruments, and to force instrumentalists to play better. Copland gives several specific examples of Berlioz's "orchestral daring."

226. "Our Younger Generation Ten Years Later." *Modern Music,* 13 (May–June 1936): 3–11. (Reprint—"1936: America's Young Men—Ten Years Later." In *Copland on Music.*)

Copland revisits the list of seventeen composers given ten years earlier in "America's Young Men of Promise" (George Antheil, Avery Claflin, Henry Cowell, Herbert Elwell, Howard Hanson, Roy Harris, Richard Hammond, Quinto Maganini, Douglas Moore, Edmund Pendleton, Quincy Porter, Bernard Rogers, Roger Sessions, Alexander Steinert, Leo Sowerby, Randall Thompson, and Virgil Thomson). Copland discusses whether those named constituted a school of American composers and constructs four categories—from prominent to obscure—into which he places the composers. He also creates a new list of young composers, dividing them into groups by ages of under twenty-five, about twenty-five, and over twenty-five (Henry Brant, David Diamond, and Norman Cazden; Robert McBride, Jerome Moross, Paul Bowles, Hunter Johnson, and Samuel Barber; and Marc Blitzstein, Israel Citkowitz, Gerald Strang, Ross Lee Finney, Elie Siegmeister, Irwin Heilner, Lehman Engel, Paul Creston, and Edwin Gershefski).

227. "Outline of History (Nef)." n.d. MS. 201/5, Aaron Copland Collection. Music Division, Library of Congress, Washington, DC.

This is a rather lengthy handwritten outline of music history from antiquity to polyphonic music in France during the eleventh through fourteenth centuries.

228. "Paris: 1928."

See: "European Festivals and Premieres: A Glance Backward" and "Stravinsky's *Oedipus Rex.*"

229. "Performers and New Music." *The Sunday Times Magazine* [London], 12 October 1958, p. 20. (Reprint—"Interpreters and New Music." In *Copland on Music.*)

While "world wide" programming is a "rehash of more of the same," London has a particularly "more virulent form" of this disease than elsewhere. "Apathy in the making of programs—giving the public what it wants and nothing but what it wants—leads to the complete stagnation of music as an art." Performers as a group have contributed to this "appalling sameness of repertoire" and have a responsibility to the art of music to "reanimate their interest in the whole corpus of musical literature, old and new." Virtuoso performers who have not kept abreast of contemporary music are not able to "adequately interpret the classics of the past without hearing them through the ears of the present." See: "[A Visiting Composer]."

230. "The Personality of Stravinsky." In *Igor Stravinsky.* Edited by Edwin Corle, pp. 121–122. New York: Duell, Sloan and Pearce, 1949. (Reprint—In *Igor* Stravinsky. Freeport, NY: Books for Libraries Press, 1969. 245 p. ISBN 0836911202. ML410 .S932C77 1969. Also Reprint as portion of—"The Composer: Igor Stravinsky." In *Copland on Music.*)

The essence of Igor Stravinsky's musical personality is difficult to describe, despite its being "one of the most individual natures of our time." Stravinsky's music "invariably sounds like music that only he could have written." In his most recent works—sober and generally lacking "sensuous appeal"—"thought and instinct are inextricably wedded, as they should be."

231. "[Phonograph Recordings]." n.d. MS. 201/7, Aaron Copland Collection. Music Division, Library of Congress, Washington, DC.

When an "authentic" version of a composition is captured on a recording, a composer tends to regard it primarily as a "standard of reference" for later performers. "The worst thing one can say about a recorded work is that the performance—good or bad—is always the same . . . Permanency turns out to be a bore." Copland then recounts glaring inaccuracies on various recordings of his compositions. He concludes that the copyright law of 1909 failed to protect composers from injustices in the recording industry.

232. "The Pianist: William Kapell."

See: "The Measure of Kapell."

233. "Piano Fantasy by Aaron Copland." 1957. MS. 201/8, Aaron Copland Collection. Music Division, Library of Congress, Washington, DC.

See: "Fantasy for Piano: Composer Explains Its Particular Problems."

234. "Piano Fantasy—Comments by Mr. Copland." 20 March 1972. Program notes, Eastern Michigan University, Department of Music, Ypsilanti, Michigan. Dady Mehta, pianist.

These program notes were excerpted from "Piano Fantasy by Aaron Copland." In the notes, Copland focuses on the history of the composition, its formal structures, and his adaptation of the twelve-tone technique.

235. "Piano Music of Noël Lee." n.d. MS. 201/10, Aaron Copland Collection. Music Division, Library of Congress, Washington, DC.

In this two-paragraph handwritten draft, Copland comments on Noël Lee's compositional style—"always a *musical* pleasure" to listen to because "music to him is a natural language, a language he uses without strain or mannerism." Lee's piano music is "especially persuasive" since he was an "accomplished instrumentalist." Copland concludes: "Once a piece begins the ear won't let go, it follows in to the very end."

236. "Pioneer Listener." Review of *Discoveries of a Music Critic,* by Paul Rosenfeld. *New Republic,* 15 April 1936, pp. 291–292.

Copland reviews Paul Rosenfeld's *Discoveries of a Music Critic,* a book of essays on topics ranging from Claudio Monteverdi through the "latest moderns." For Copland, Rosenfeld was an unusual critic: "He listens to music primarily because he loves it, and he writes about it primarily because he wishes to communicate what he has experienced while listening." Copland critiques Rosenfeld's stance on Igor Stravinsky, Henry Cowell, and American opera.

237. "Playing Safe at Zurich." *Modern Music,* 4 (November–December 1926): 28–31. (Reprint—"Zurich: 1926." In *Copland on Music.*)

The fourth festival of the International Society for Contemporary Music presented works that neither were a great success nor contained revelations. Copland compares the compositions by French and German composers, concluding that the Germans made the "better showing." He is particularly complimentary of works by Paul Hindemith, Anton Webern, and William Walton, at the same time quickly dismissing a concerto by Kurt Weill. Copland also discusses works by André Caplet, P. O. Ferroud, Walter Geiser, Arthur Hoerée, Hans Krasa, Ernst Levy, Felix Petyrek, and Arnold Schoenberg. See: "European Festivals and Premieres: A Glance Backward."

238. *The Pleasures of Music: An Address at the University of New Hampshire, April 16, 1959.* In Distinguished Lecture Series, April 1959. Durham, NH: University of New Hampshire, 1959. 23 p. ML3847 .C6. (Reprint—"The Pleasures of Music," *Saturday Evening Post,* 4 July 1959, pp. 19, 38, 42, 44. Also Reprint—"The Pleasures of Music." In *Copland on Music.*)

This article was originally an address given (on 16 April 1959) as part of the Distinguished Lecture Series at the University of New Hampshire. Speaking as a composer rather than an author, Copland examines "the varied pleasures to be derived from experiencing music as an art." While music strikes both passive listener and trained musician with a similar immediacy, the musician's understanding increases musical pleasure. Attempting to increase such understanding for the general listener, Copland discusses the contributions of rhythm and tone color to the musical flow that moves all listeners. Copland also considers the specific pleasures gained from listening to compositions by J. S. Bach, Ludwig van Beethoven, Giovanni Palestrina, Arnold Schoenberg, Giuseppe Verdi, and even imperfect compositions. (The version published in the *Saturday Evening Post* is slightly abbreviated from the University of New

Hampshire speech—and its reprint in *Copland on Music*—focusing less on the early and modern music examples.)

239. "Portrait of a Symphony." n.d. MS. 201/13, Aaron Copland Collection. Music Division, Library of Congress, Washington, DC.

This is the handwritten manuscript for the foreword to *Portrait of a Symphony.* See: Foreword to *Portrait of a Symphony.*

240. Preface to *Composers, Conductors, and Critics,* by Claire R. Reis, pp. v–vi (Detroit: Detroit Reprints in Music, 1974). xvi, xiii, 264 p. ISBN 0911772626. ML423 .R365A3 1974.

In the foreword to Claire Reis's *Composers, Conductors, and Critics,* Copland briefly summarizes Reis's role as executive director of the League of Composers and her staunch support "of the interests of the living composer." Reis's book chronicles the development of "the new music" between 1923 and 1948. Copland concludes that the "scene has changed, but the cause remains the same: how to make way for the new voice—the truly creative voice in our contemporary musical world."

241. "The Present Day."

    See: "The Musical Scene Changes."

242. "Previously Unpublished Composers' Letters As Written to Claire R. Reis."

See: "Composers' Letters."

243. "Problemes de la musique de film." *La vie musicale,* 1 (March 1951): 5–6.

This citation is unverified.

244. "A Quarter-Century Reflection." *American Composers Alliance Bulletin,* 11 (December 1963): 1.

The American Composers Alliance was founded twenty-five years earlier in an attempt to obtain "just remuneration" and wider recognition for the American composer. Reflecting on its quarter-century of existence, Copland notes: "The establishment of the ACA marked the end of the Age of Innocence for the American composer. It gave him a new sense of pride in his profession, and a new urgency as to the need for group action."

245. "Questions on Music." n.d. MS. 201/15, Aaron Copland Collection. Music Division, Library of Congress, Washington, DC.

"Questions on Music" appears to be a typed multiple choice and short answer music appreciation-style quiz. In it Copland asks questions on conductors, composers, symphony orchestras, instrumental families of the orchestra, Bach's three most famous sons, meters for specific dances, Latin American musical terms, and Broadway and film composers.

246. "Ralph Hawkes: In Memorium." 1950. MS. 201/16, Aaron Copland Collection. Music Division, Library of Congress, Washington, DC.

This folder includes a pencil draft accompanied by a printed obituary that does not seem to be a result of the pencil draft. In the draft, Copland speculates on the role of the publisher/businessman in contemporary musical America. In the printed obituary, Ralph Hawkes's musical contributions as publisher (Boosey & Hawkes), musical instrument manufacturer, musical activist, and promoter and supporter of the Sadler's Wells [Ballet] Company and Covent Garden Royal Opera House were outlined. Hawkes was "a leading pioneer in the field of contemporary music and a strong force not only in publishing the works of contemporary composers, but also in organized movements for the protection of the composers' interests."

247. "Report on American Music, 1956." 1956. MS. 201/16, Aaron Copland Collection. Music Division, Library of Congress, Washington, DC.

This is the typescript draft for "American Culture I: Music, 1956." See: "American Culture I: Music, 1956" and "Serious Music Serious Problem: Few Can Name the Tune."

248. "Review of Benjamin Britten's *The Rape of Lucretia*."

See: "Benjamin Britten: *The Rape of Lucretia,* an Opera in Two Acts."

249. "The Role of the Composer/Le rôle du compositeur." *Canadian Composer,* 63 (October 1971): 24–35.

This article is an edited text from Copland's CAPAC-Sir Ernest MacMillan lecture, which he had recently delivered at the University of Toronto. He compares the role of the contemporary composer working in industrial America to that of the European composer working within a more supportive musical superstructure. The difficulty of expressing the human condition through music is putting "non-essential feelings . . . into some usable, understandable form." While reviewing changes since the beginning of the century, Copland discusses musical advances, varying relationships between composer and audience, and democratization of the musical environment through electronics. The concerns Copland expresses about composing in a scientific age parallel statements in "New Electronic Media." See: "New Electronic Media."

250. "Rubin Goldmark: A Tribute." *Juilliard Review,* 3 (Fall 1956): 15–16.

Copland presented these remarks at the dedication ceremony for The Goldmark Wing at The City College of New York. Rubin Goldmark, Copland's former teacher and first chair of composition at Juilliard School of Music, was among the "prime founders" of the brilliant musical future of the United States. His most important contributions were made as a teacher rather than as a composer. Copland concluded that Goldmark was "a true American and a true citizen of the Republic of Music."

251. "Salute to the Arts and Artists of Latin America." 1967. MS. 201/19, Aaron Copland Collection. Music Division, Library of Congress, Washington, DC.

In this one-page typed salutation to the artists of Latin America, Copland states: "The love of art in all its many forms is indubitably one of the greatest of forces for bringing together all mankind." This greeting is an expression of solidarity with the Latin American artist, who, like the North American, was involved in the process of creating an art "expressive of our own time and of the deepest aspirations of the Western world . . . What the European artist has accomplished for the old world we must accomplish for the new."

252. "A Salute to Schwann." n.d. MS. 201/20, Aaron Copland Collection. Music Division, Library of Congress, Washington, DC.

In this article, written for the twenty-fifth anniversary of the Schwann Record Catalogue, Copland extolls the bibliographic wonders of the collection. He notes how the catalog reflected contemporary thought on composers: Erik Satie's "modest output has flowered on these pages," while the "unfairly neglected" Darius Milhaud garnered a "mere half a column of a dozen works."

253. "Scherchen on Conducting and Ewen on Composers." Review of *Handbook of Conducting,* by Hermann Scherchen and *Composers of Today,* by David Ewen. *Modern Music,* 12 (January–February 1935): 94-96.

In this article, Copland reviews two books: *Handbook of Conducting* by Hermann Scherchen and *Composers of Today* by David Ewen. Copland seems ultimately convinced by Scherchen's argument that "a student can be fully prepared for his job as conductor without ever having faced an orchestra"—an idea contrary to conventional theory. Copland states that "whatever can be learned" about the technique of orchestral conducting, "this book teaches." Ewen's book, however, "is full of inaccuracies, one or more to the page," and "is not to be taken too seriously." Copland lists several of these inaccuracies.

254. "*Schoenberg and His School,* by René Leibowitz."

See: "The World of A-Tonality." Review of *Schoenberg and His School,* by René Leibowitz.

255. "Scores and Records." *Modern Music,* 14 (November–December 1936): 39–42.

"Scores and Records," written for the "increasing army of record fans," was one of five new departments that first appeared in this issue. Copland lauds R. D. Darrell for his compilation *Gramophone Shop Encyclopedia of Recorded Music,* in which Darrell, among other things, confronted record companies with "the inaccuracy of their own labels." Among the scores and records Copland reviews and discusses are works by Béla Bartók, Georges Enesco, Jean Françaix, Paul Hindemith, Gian Malipiero, Darius Milhaud, Francis Poulenc, Florent Schmitt, Jean Sibelius, Igor Stravinsky, and Alexandre Tansman.

256. "Scores and Records." *Modern Music,* 14 (January–February 1937): 98–101.

In this article from the series "Scores and Records," Copland marvels that music publishers continue to print new music, when the buying public has little interest in the scores and the potential buyers do not have the money. He also notes that G. Schirmer had begun to offer miniature study scores. In this installment, Copland reviews compositions by Samuel Barber, Carlos Chávez, Anis Fuleihan, Paul Hindemith, Emil Hlobil, Paul Nordoff, Arnold Schoenberg, Max Springer, and Léo Weiner.

257. "Scores and Records." *Modern Music,* 14 (March–April 1937): 167–170.

In this "Scores and Records" Copland announces the formation of the Brunswick-Polydor label, which released Alban Berg's *Lyric Suite* ("the first representative work of the Viennese school" to be recorded), Albert Roussel's Symphony No. 3, and Igor Stravinsky's Concerto in D Major—all of which he reviews. He also reviews or announces releases of compositions by Jacob Avshalomov, Copland, Claude Debussy, Max Kowalski, Charles Martin Loeffler, Darius Milhaud, and Sergei Prokofiev. Among the scores, Copland reviews works by William H. Bailey, Conrad Beck, Mildred Couper, and Felix Petyrek.

258. "Scores and Records." *Modern Music,* 14 (May–June 1937): 230–233.

In this installment from the series "Scores and Records," Copland questions whether huge profit-making record companies did not "owe some ethical debt to the future of the art of music." In the previous quarter, for example, RCA Victor had released only a single record of contemporary music. Among the composers and compositions Copland discusses are Frederick Delius, Paul Hindemith, Charles Ives, Walter Piston, Francis Poulenc, Maurice Ravel, Nino Rota, William Walton, and Ralph Vaughan Williams.

259. "Scores and Records." *Modern Music,* 15 (November–December 1937): 45–48.

Among the recordings that Copland reviews are Gustav Mahler's *Das Lied von der Erde,* Jean Sibelius's Sixth Symphony and *String Quartet, Voces intimea,* Gian Francesco Malipiero's *Rispetti e strombotti,* Vittorio Rieti's Quartet in F Major, Arthur Honegger's *Judith,* and Francis Poulenc's *Le bestiaire.* Copland reviews scores by Igor Stravinsky (*Jeu de cartes*), Zoltán Kodály (*Te Deum*), Mario Castelnuovo-Tedesco (two concertos), and Paul White (*Sinfonietta for String Orchestra*). Copland predicts that the future of American music lies between the music of William Grant Still and Otto Cesano on the one hand, and Otto Luening and Gerald Strang on the other.

260. "Scores and Records." *Modern Music,* 15 (January–February 1938): 109–111.

In the absence of new recordings of modern music released during the holidays, Copland reviews current swing bands (Bunny Berrigan, Tommy Dorsey, Duke Ellington, Benny Goodman, Raymond Scott, Joe Usifer, and "Fats" Waller). Copland criticizes compositions by Henry Brant, Edwin Gershefski, and Gerald Strang as being "strangely unrelated to any American feeling, and [giving] their composers an aura of isolation which is deadly." Copland also reviews scores by Frederick Converse, Arthur Shepherd, and Albert Stoessel.

261. "Scores and Records." *Modern Music,* 15 (March–April 1938): 179–182.

Among the scores that Copland reviews for this installment are *Summer's Last Will and Testament* (Constant Lambert, text by Thomas Nashe), Symphony in F Minor (Ralph Vaughan Williams), *The Cradle Will Rock* (Marc Blitzstein), Toccata and *Prelude and Blues* (Conlon Nancarrow), *United Quartet* (Henry Cowell), and *Two Symphonic Interludes* (Otto Luening). Among the new record releases that Copland reviews are *Opéras-minutes* (Darius Milhaud), Sonata for cello and piano (Pierre Octave Ferroud),

Indianisches Tagebuch (Ferruccio Busoni), Suite for saxophone and piano (Paul Creston), *Warm-up* and *Let-down* (Robert McBride), and *Study* (Harrison Kerr).

262. "Scores and Records." *Modern Music,* 15 (May–June 1938): 244–248.

Among the scores that Copland reviews are Violin Concerto (Roger Sessions), *In Honour of the City of London* (William Walton), Mass (Francis Poulenc), *Pioneers* (William Schuman), *Psalm* (David Diamond), *Contrasts and Developments* (Nicholas Nabokoff), and Sonata for violin and piano (Edmund Rubbra). Among the records reviewed by Copland are a set of Hindu music by Uday Shan-Kar's Company of Musicians and Dancers, Symphony in F Minor (Ralph Vaughan Williams), *The Triumph of Neptune* (Lord Berners), *Symphony for Voices* (Roy Harris), *Octandre* (Edgar Varèse), and *Fugato on a Well-Known Theme* (Robert McBride).

263. "Scores and Records." *Modern Music,* 16 (November–December 1938): 50–54.

In this installment, Copland reviews the following scores: *Mathis der Maler, Nobilissima visione,* and *Symphonic Dances* (Paul Hindemith), commenting on their connection to World War II Germany; *I've Got the Tune* (Marc Blitzstein), *Variations on a Theme of Frank Bridge* (Benjamin Britten), and *Sérénade concertante* (Marcel Dellanoy). Among the records Copland reviewed were *The Program of Piano Music* and the suite from *Lieutenant Kijé* (Sergei Prokofiev), Fifth Symphony and *Pohjola's Daughter* (Jean Sibelius), *Music for Strings* (Arthur Bliss), Concerto for piano and orchestra (Jean Françaix), *Cantari alla Madrigalesca* (Gian Malipiero), and *Ronsard à son âme* and *Don Quichotte à Dulcinée* (Maurice Ravel). Copland stresses the cultural responsibility of record companies as part of their business enterprise.

264. "Scores and Records." *Modern Music,* 16 (January–February 1939): 122–125.

Among the recently released recordings, Copland reviews the String Quartet in D Major, Opus 45 (Albert Roussel), *Pictures at an Exhibition,* arranged by Lucien Cailliet (Modest Mussorgsky), Violin

Sonata (Ernest Bloch), *St. Paul's Suite* (Gustav Holst), *Cafe sin nombre* and *Huapangos* (Paul Bowles), excerpts from *114 Songs* (Charles Ives), excerpts from Suite for clarinet and bassoon (Johanna Beyer), and *Two Chorales and Ostinato* (Henry Cowell). Among the scores reviewed are Symphony (Harold Morris), String Quartet, No. 3 (Karol Rathaus), *John Henry* (Elie Siegmeister), *Hot Stuff (We Hope)* (Robert McBride), and *Amarus* and *Intimate Pages* (Leoš Janáček). Copland also lists piano works by James Cleghorn, Belle Fenstock, Leopold Godowsky, Lou Harrison, Gian-Carlo Menotti, Maurice Ravel, William Reddick, Arthur Schwarzwald, and Julia Smith.

265. "Search for an 'American' Music." *Music and Musicians*, 9 (September 1960): 15.

In this continuation from "Making Music in the Star-Spangled Manner," Copland discusses his attraction to jazz rhythms in the 1920s, the presence of field recordings to inspire the use of folk materials, his modifications of folk materials into thematic materials, and the career of Roy Harris. See: from "Making Music in the Star-Spangled Manner" and the continuations of the article "A Businessman Who Wrote Music on Sundays" and "America's Young Men of Music."

266. "Second Thoughts on Hollywood." *Modern Music*, 17 (March–April 1940): 141–147. (Reprint—"Music in the Films." In *Our New Music*. Also Reprint—"Music in the Films." In *The Music Lover's Handbook*. Edited by Elie Siegmeister, pp. 628–635. New York: W. Morrow, 1943. xiii, 817 p. ML55 .S6.)

In Hollywood—where the living composer is "actually needed"—"music is like a small flame put under the screen to help warm it." Copland discusses the two issues that make a Hollywood composer happy: "the producer you work for, and the amount of time allotted for completing the score." (You must write to please the producer, and most scores must be completed in two weeks.) He then lists three ways that music helps a film: "The first is by intensifying the emotional impact of any given scene, the second by creating an illusion of continuity and the third by providing a kind of neutral background music." Among the overused conventions of Hollywood film scores

are the inevitability of the "late nineteenth-century symphonic style,"
the use of leitmotifs for characters rather than underlying narrative
themes, and the "'Mickey-Mousing'" of the action. Copland retraces
the steps by which music is added to a film and called on music critics
to elevate the art of film music by drawing attention to "ambitious"
scores. Finally, he discusses the works of specific Hollywood composers: Anthony Collins, Werner Janssen, Erich Korngold, Alfred
Newman, Max Steiner, Ernst Toch, and Victor Young.

267. "Serge Koussevitzky and the American Composer." *Musical
    Quarterly*, 30 (July 1944): 255–261. (Reprint—"The Con-
    ductor: Serge Koussevitzky." In *Copland on Music*.)

For two decades—a period that corresponded to the coming of age
of the American symphonic literature—conductor Sergey Koussevitzky carried out a policy of performing orchestral works by
American composers. Among Koussevitzky's earliest "protégés,"
Copland tells of his initial meeting and subsequent performances
under the conductor. Copland describes the "specialness" of a
Koussevitzky premiere, the result of the conductor's total commitment to the preparation of the work and the conviction of the
resultant performance. Koussevitzky possessed a daily preoccupation with the subsistence of the living composer and an "unwaver-
ing belief in the musical creative force," which led him to establish
the Koussevitzky Music Foundation to commission new compositions.

268. "Serious Music Serious Problem: Few Can Name the Tune."
    Democrat & Chronicle [Rochester, NY], 15 July 1956, sec. F,
    p. 1.

See: "American Culture I: Music, 1956," "Report on American
Music, 1956," "El compositor en los Estados Unidos," and "The
Composer in the United States."

269. "Shönberg and His School."

See: "A World of A-Tonality."

270. "Shop Talk: On the Notation of Rhythm."

See: "On the Notation of Rhythm."

271. "Sobre la música en el cine." n.d. MS. 202/2, Aaron Copland Collection. Music Division, Library of Congress, Washington, DC.

This is an abridged version of "Tip to Moviegoers: Take Off Those Ear-Muffs," printed in *Buenos Aires Musical.* (No other bibliographic information given.)

272. "Some Notes on My *Music for the Theatre.*" *Victor Record Review,* 3 (March 1941): 6, 18, 21.

At the time that the article was written, *Music for the Theatre* was Copland's most frequently performed composition. Copland details the reception history of *Music for the Theatre,* including the "mild *succes de scandale*" at its premiere under conductor Sergey Koussevitzky, and varying critical responses following subsequent performances in the United States, France, and Germany. In retrospect, Copland remembers *Music for the Theatre* as a "*jugend-werk,* with all that that implies of youthful enthusiasm and unhackneyed ideas." See: "*Music for the Theatre.*"

273. "South American Journey," 1947. MS. 202/4, Aaron Copland Collection. Music Division, Library of Congress, Washington, DC.

This is a manuscript draft for "Composer's Report on Music in South America." See: "Composer's Report on Music in South America."

274. "Special Fondness for B.B. [Benjamin Britten]." n.d. MS. 202/5, Aaron Copland Collection. Music Division, Library of Congress, Washington, DC.

Copland's fondness for Benjamin Britten shows in his descriptions of the British composer: "By present-day standards he is musically a conservative—but his musical impulse is so spontaneous and winning that the matter of the style he chooses to work in becomes secondary and the attractiveness of the music itself is the compelling thing." Copland describes Britten's music as having an "extraordinary flair—a dashing sureness of technique." Copland concludes that Britten "begins with a wonderful asset—the ability to plan out a work in its entirety and in its every detail—could have made a city planner of genius."

275. "Stadium Concert."

See: "The Composer Speaks Out! Meet the Composer!" and "The Live Composer."

276. "Stefan Wolpe (1948)."

See: "Stefan Wolpe: Two Songs for Alto and Piano from *The Song of Songs.*"

277. "Stefan Wolpe: Two Songs for Alto and Piano from *The Song of Songs.*" *Music Library Association Notes,* 2d ser., 6 (December 1948): 172. (Reprint—"Stefan Wolpe [1948]." In *Copland on Music.*)

The music of Stefan Wolpe, "one of the most remarkable of living composers," is generally unknown in the United States because it is "grimly serious," stark, and uncompromising. Although only two songs, these works are "exceptional"—"intensely alive, deeply Jewish, and very personal." "Wolpe's music is strikingly original, with a kind of fiery inner logic that makes for fascinated listening . . . It is a sad commentary on the state of our musical house that this man must create in comparative isolation."

278. "The Story behind *El Salón México.*" *Victor Record Review,* 1 (April 1939): 4-5.

This history of *El Salón México* was written to accompany the release of its recording by the Boston Symphony Orchestra under Sergey Koussevitzky. Copland provides a colorful description of the *Salón México* and its inspiration of the composition for which it was named. It was at this dance hall that Copland felt a "really live contact" with the Mexican people—"their humanity, their separate shyness, their dignity and unique charm." He also discusses the origins and compositional issues involved in the use of the Mexican tunes, in addition to the performance history of *El Salón México.*

279. "Stravinsky and Hindemith Premieres." *Modern Music,* 9 (January–February 1932): 85–88. (Reprint abridged— "Berlin: 1932." In *Copland on Music.* Reprint Stravinsky section—*Stravinsky in Modern Music [1924–1946].* Compiled

by Carol J. Oja. New York: Da Capo Press, 1982. xix, 176 p.
ISBN 0306761084. ML410 .S932S793 1982.)

In 1931 Berlin, the only musical rival to New York City, hosted the premieres of Igor Stravinsky's Violin Concerto and Paul Hindemith's oratorio, *Das Unaufhörliche.* In reviewing Stravinsky's Violin Concerto, Copland refutes the "myth" that Stravinsky "adopted a new style with each new work" and explains his neoclassical "manner" up to that point. Disappointed that the Violin Concerto lacked Stravinsky's typical "seriousness of tone," Copland questions whether this was the "first indication Stravinsky has given of a weakening of his powers." Hindemith's setting of Gottfried Benn's text about the "Life Force" contained an "overwhelmingly conventional note that spoiled whatever merit the separate solos and choruses had." Copland also reviews compositions by Ferruccio Busoni and Jerzy Fitelberg.

280. "Stravinsky's *Oedipus Rex.*" *New Republic,* 29 February 1928, 68–69. (Reprint abridged—"Paris: 1928." In *Copland on Music.*)

Copland explains the cold reception of *Oedipus rex,* by conservatives and modernists alike, based on Igor Stravinsky's apparent "about-face" of neoclassicism following *The Rite of Spring.* Copland argues that Stravinsky's gradual move from realism to objectivism created a "clear unity of esthetic purpose in all his production, from *Petrushka* to *Oedipus Rex.*" Understanding that Stravinsky's move to rid music of the inherited nineteenth-century romanticism, helps the listener "better appreciate the revolutionary gesture of Stravinsky in returning to the impersonal ideals of the eighteenth century." Copland discusses Stravinsky's "self-imposed limitations" of neoclassicism in *Oedipus Rex* and predicts that the Neoclassical movement will become "tempered by some compromise with romanticism."

281. "Talk on N. B. [Nadia Boulanger]." n.d. MS. 202/9, Aaron Copland Collection. Music Division, Library of Congress, Washington, DC.

This is a handwritten draft outline of topics to discuss about Nadia Boulanger. The topics closely follow other printed statements about

Boulanger's musical importance, teaching environment, personality, and biography.

282. "Tanglewood's Future: Measures to Insure Continuity Include Extensive New Scholarship Program." *New York Times,* 24 February 1952, sec. 2, p. 7 (Reprint—"Tanglewood: 1952." *Tempo,* 24 [Summer 1952]: 22–23. Also—Reprint "Tanglewood's Future: Measures to Insure Continuity Include Extensive New Scholarship Program." *Berkshire Music Center,* 10th Session [June 30–August 10 1952], n.p.)

Ten years after the Berkshire Music Center was founded, Copland reminisced on its accomplishments and announced its initiatives for the future. To ensure that the late Sergey Koussevitzky's dream would be continued, a faculty board—including Copland—and a music director were appointed by the Boston Symphony Orchestra's Board of Trustees. Plans to "broaden the base of the school, enlarge its usefulness in the musical scene, and to extend its influence to all parts of the musical world" included a tuition waiver scholarship for certain departments, the formation of the Tanglewood Study Group for the "intelligent amateur and music enthusiast," and the opening of the chamber music and song repertoire divisions.

283. "The Teacher: Nadia Boulanger." 1960. MS. 202/11, Aaron Copland Collection. Music Division, Library of Congress, Washington, DC.

This typescript was published as "Nadia Boulanger: An Affectionate Portrait" and "The Teacher: Nadia Boulanger" in *Copland on Music.* See: "Nadia Boulanger: An Affectionate Portrait."

284. "Thomson and Blitzstein."

See: "Marc Blitzstein."

285. "Thomson's Musical State." Review of *The State of Music,* by Virgil Thomson. *Modern Music,* 17 (October–November 1939): 63–65. (Reprint—"Virgil Thomson's Musical State." In *Copland on Music.*)

Copland found Virgil Thomson's *The State of Music* to be "the wittiest, the most provocative, the best written, the least conventional book on matters musical that I have ever seen." The book is especially important for composers, since "for once the composer is treated as a human being, with not merely a craftman's interest, but also economic, political, and social interests." Among Thomson's topics are "professional solidarity" among composers, "the economic determinism of musical style," the compositional problems of various genres, the "dissonant-contrapuntal" International style in modern music, and the composer as a "miniature capitalist" and "political animal."

286. "Threnody—Igor Stravinsky: In Memoriam."

See: "In Memoriam Igor Stravinsky: Canons & Epitaphs—Set 2."

287. "Tip to Moviegoers: Take Off Those Ear-Muffs." *New York Times Magazine,* 6 November 1949, pp. 28–32. (Reprint— "Film Music." In *What to Listen for in Music.*)

This critical guide to compositional techniques and elements of movie music was written by Copland to encourage critical listening in movie audiences. In this article, he defends movie scores as legitimate art music, enumerating both the pitfalls and the possibilities that this new musical medium brought to the field of composition. Copland documents the current steps of adding a musical sound track to a motion picture and described six functions of music within a movie score. See: "Music and the Movies," "La musica per film: nuovo mezzo di espressione musicale," and "Sobre la música en el cine."

288. "A Tribute to Franz Liszt." *HiFi/Stereo Review,* 5 (October 1960): 46–49. (Reprint—"Liszt as Pioneer." In *Copland on Music.*)

In assessing Franz Liszt's contributions, Copland states that it was Liszt who weakened the hegemony of German music, advancing the "rise of nationalism as a musical ideal." Copland admires Liszt's embodiment of his epoch, his prolific output, and his ability to identify the "mature composer in the embryonic stage." Musically, Liszt foreshadowed the twentieth century with his choice of sonorities and their spacing, his harmonic vocabulary of unsuspected modulations and chord progressions, and his development of the symphonic poem with its thematic metamorphoses. For these reasons Copland states: "We do him and ourselves a grave injustice in ignoring the scope of his work and the profound influence it has exerted on the contemporary scene." See: "Franz Liszt."

289. "A Tribute to Nadia Boulanger." 1967. MS. 202/13, Aaron Copland Collection. Music Division, Library of Congress, Washington, DC.

This article, a tribute to Nadia Boulanger on her eightieth birthday, was written for the Associated Press and carried under various titles. "For sixty years she has uninterruptedly guided the musical training of hundreds of young people," rising "to the top of her profession in a field dominated by men, and without herself engaging in a career as a composer." Boulanger possessed two crucial qualities as an outstanding teacher: "She knows all the answers to any troubling technical question, and she instills in the fledgling composer, when convinced of his gift, a sense of confidence in his own powers, even before they have been put to any serious test." Copland discusses Boulanger's American pupils and Lili Boulanger's career, in addition to his more typical description of Boulanger's studio, personality, and the Wednesday sessions, followed by teas with the "musical elite" of Paris.

Also carried under the following titles on 3 September 1967:
"Aaron Copland Remembers Nadia." *The Courier-Journal and Times* [Louisville, KY].
"Famous Pupil Recalls Famous Teacher." *Chicago Sun-Times*.
"A Famous Pupil Remembers: Song of Praise to a Music Teacher." *The Sunday Bulletin* [Philadelphia].
"Her Best Pupils Are Famous: Aaron Copland Pays Tribute to Teacher of Musical Composition, Nadia Boulanger, Who Rose to Top in a Man's World." *The Milwaukee Journal.*
"Mlle. Boulanger and Her Bakery." *Houston Chronicle.*
"Mlle. Boulanger, 80 This Month, Has Taught Greatest Composers." *The Springfield Sunday Republican* [Springfield, MA].
"Musical World Honors Teacher Nadia Boulanger." *Sunday Telegram* [No city identified].
"Nadia Boulanger at 80 Still Foremost Music Teacher." *The Battle Creek Enquirer and News.*
"Nadia Boulanger, Master Teacher: She Fans Musical Spark." [Clipping without citation.]

"Paris Octogenarian Is a Musical Marvel." *Times-Dispatch*. [Full title missing.]

"She Has Taught the Greatest . . ." *Rochester Democrat and Chronicle*.

"She Taught Many of the World's Best Musicians." *The Rocky Mount [NC] Telegram*.

"The Tutor of Eminent Composers, Mlle. Boulanger Going Strong at 79." *Arkansas Gazette*.

290. "Tributes and Reminiscences: Aaron Copland." In *Michael Tippett: A Symposium on His 60th Birthday*. Edited by Ian Kemp, p. 53. London: Faber and Faber, 1965. ML 410 .T467K4.

Although British, Michael Tippett possessed an American quality in both his music and personality. For Copland, it was this "amalgamation of the familiar and the foreign that constitutes his special charm." The "Americanness" of Tippett's personality—outgoing, spirited, and enthusiastic—made him "cousin" to American composers. Musically, Tippett's "Americanness" was expressed in his "directness of expression, his clear-cut themes," and his "familiarity with and a fondness for American-derived rhythm"—syncopation, cross-rhythms, and asymmetricality. See: "Cousin Michael."

291. "Twentieth Century: Reorientation and Experiment." In *Music and Western Man: The Canadian Broadcasting Corporation*. Edited by Peter Garvie, pp. 281–285. New York: Philosophical Library, 1958. xxiii, 328 p. ML55 .M66.

In this article, Copland discusses the contributions of Claude Debussy, Charles Ives, Gustav Mahler, Modest Mussorgsky, Arnold Schoenberg, Richard Strauss, and Igor Stravinsky to the technical and aesthetic revolution of the twentieth century. Copland identifies one piece (and its recording) that best typifies each composer's contribution.

292. "U.S. Books and Music: A Vital and Varied Music." n.d. MS. 230/3, Aaron Copland Collection. Music Division, Library of Congress, Washington, DC.

The majority of this article is two-sentence reviews, organized by genre, of recordings of significant American compositions. Each entry generally includes names of composer, composition, orchestra, conductor, recording label, and number, in addition to a brief synopsis. Copland credits the long-playing record with attracting "widespread attention" to American art music. For Copland, this list proves that Americanism in music is not limited to the use of jazz materials, but is "the attempt to reflect in musical terms the deepest and most significant aspects of American life, the full range of American civilization." See: "American Composers on Records" and "A Vital and Varied Music."

293. "A Verdict." In *Paul Rosenfeld, Voyager in the Arts.*

See: "Memorial to Paul Rosenfeld."

294. "Virgil Thomson's Musical State."

See: "Thomson's Musical State."

295. "A Visit to Israel," 1969. MS. 202/14, Aaron Copland Collection. Music Division, Library of Congress, Washington, DC.

These manuscripts are drafts for "Aaron Copland: A Visit to Israel." See: "Aaron Copland: A Visit to Israel."

296. "A Visit to Snape." In *Tribute to Benjamin Britten on His Fiftieth Birthday.* Edited by Anthony Gishford, pp. 71–73. London: Faber and Faber, 1963, 195 p. ML55 .B75G6 1963.

In this birthday tribute, Copland describes his initial meeting with Benjamin Britten and his music and the reasons for their camaraderie as young composers with a shared "affinity" of musical interests. What Copland remembered best from this meeting was "the exchange of musical impressions of all sorts." Copland played proofs of his *Second Hurricane* for Britten, who subsequently developed a "preoccupation with young voices." In return, Copland critiqued the substance of Britten's Piano Concerto No. 1, his frankness ultimately cementing their friendship.

297. "[A Visiting Composer]." 1958. MS. 202/16, Aaron Copland Collection. Music Division, Library of Congress, Washington, DC.

This is the manuscript for "Performers and New Music." See: "Performers and New Music."

298. "A Vital and Varied Music." n.d. MS. 230/3, Aaron Copland Collection. Music Division, Library of Congress, Washington, DC.

   See: "U.S. Books and Music: A Vital and Varied Music."

299. "What Europe Means to the Aspiring Composer." *Musical America*, 3 January 1925, pp. 15, 27.

In this article Copland, recently returned from his studies in Paris, writes about a hypothetical American composer who traveled to Europe to apply the "finishing touch" to his musical education. In answering the question whether European training is essential for an American composer, Copland states that "European methods are unnecessarily stringent, while in comparison with them American methods are too lax." He carefully details the thorough musical training of European conservatories and the inadequacies felt by an American student, concluding: "It is difficult to see how we can develop [an educational] standard until we have a national conservatory based approximately on the principles which govern the most famous conservatories of Europe."

300. "What Is Jewish Music?" Review of *The Music of Israel,* by Peter Gradenwitz. *New York Herald Tribune,* 2 October 1949, sec. 7, p. 14.

This review is most notable for Copland's responses to Peter Gradenwitz's book as a Jewish-American composer. He expresses disappointment in the lack of information about the first "few thousand years" of Jewish music history, claimed to be covered by the author. He also questions Gradenwitz's choice of Ernest Bloch, rather than Darius Milhaud, as best expressing Jewishness in the European milieu. Copland was most interested in the section on resident Israeli composers "building a foundation for an indigenous art of the future" and in the "fairly complete listing of music inspired by the Bible."

301. "When Private and Public Worlds Meet." *New York Times,* 9 June 1968, sec. 2, p. 17.

Copland identifies the distinct talents and temperaments required of composers and conductors, stating that few (except Leonard Bernstein and Lukas Foss) were equally adept at each discipline. Both composers and conductors can learn much from the unique perspective each brings to the composer's work. Copland describes the aesthetic specific composers emphasized when conducting their own compositions (Benjamin Britten, Carlos Chávez, Paul Hindemith, Arnold Schoenberg, Richard Strauss, and Igor Stravinsky). See: "The Composer as Conductor."

302. "Where Are We? What's Been Happening to So-Called Serious Music in the Sixties." n.d. MS. 202/18, Aaron Copland Collection. Music Division, Library of Congress, Washington, DC.

In these manuscript notes for an article that was not completed, Copland questions whether electronic music is music or "a new art for which a new name should be invented." While previous generations talked of the "breakdown of music," they only referred to tonality. The post-1950s generation has put an "end to continuity in the old sense and an end to thematic relationships." Copland laments the lack of interest in symphonic music and the abandonment of an American musical voice. In conclusion, Copland writes, "electronic music—basically impressionistic in effect—no food for the mind."

303. "William Schuman (1951)."

See: "Current Chronicle: United States, New York."

304. "William Schuman: String Quartet no. 4," 1951. MS. 202/19, Aaron Copland Collection. Music Division, Library of Congress, Washington, DC.

This is the manuscript for "Current Chronicle: United States, New York." See: "Current Chronicle: United States, New York."

305. "Workers Sing!" *New Masses,* 5 June 1934, pp. 28–29.

Copland reviews the compositions in the *Worker's Song Book 1934,* "the first collection of revolutionary songs for American workers," issued by the Workers' Music League and composed by members of the Composers' Collective of the Pierre Degeyter Club of New York City. In addition to reviewing the specific compositions by Lahn Adohmyan, Janet Barnes, Carl Sands, Jacob Schaeffer, and L. E. Swift, Copland theorizes about the qualities of the mass song. (What makes a good mass song for composer and worker-singer are not necessarily the same, but musicians must insist on high musical caliber, "not for 'esthetic' reasons alone, but because a better musical setting will make a song a more thrilling experience and increase its political drive.") Copland concludes that only four of the fourteen songs represented are mass songs, the remainder "revolutionary choral compositions written for performance by trained workers' choruses and solo songs intended for concert performance."

306. "The World of A-Tonality." Review of *Schoenberg and His School,* by René Leibowitz. *New York Times,* 27 November 1949, sec. 7, p. 5. (Reprint—"Schönberg and His School [1949]." In *Copland on Music.*)

Copland describes author René Leibowitz, a Polish-born composer who studied with Arnold Schoenberg and Anton Webern, as a "born disciple, with a proselytizing fervor seldom encountered in musical treatises." Leibowitz's thesis was that contrapuntal music—which "separates our music from that of all other peoples, and gives it its special glory"—was preempted by harmony in tonal music. It was Schoenberg, in his destruction of tonality, that freed polyphony from the "harmonic hegemony." Copland criticizes Leibowitz for not mentioning "the special world—Vienna at the turn of the century—that so strongly influenced the aesthetic ideals of the music of Schönberg and his school." Copland's critique of Leibowitz's position on the twelve-tone system indicates much about Copland's reservations about the movement in general.

307. "The World of the Phonograph." *American Scholar,* 6 (1937): 27–37. (Reprint—In *Our New Music.*)

This article is important for its glimpse into the overlooked history of the phonograph. Copland outlines "intelligent" uses of the phonograph to broaden and deepen "one's entire musical experience." The phonograph, however, still had many limitations: Discs and machines were prohibitively expensive, not all ensembles or dynamics were capable of being recorded well, discs had to be changed every four-and-a-half minutes, and radio broadcasts were considered of better fidelity. Copland devises six categories of recorded music and provided illustrative examples from each: Familiar Music, Very Old Music, Very New Music, Primitive and Folk Music, Improvised Music [Jazz], and Educational Records. He also provides a bibliography of recommended recordings of familiar works, music by living composers, and music by recent composers.

308. "The Youngest Generation of American Composers." n.d. MS. 202/21, Aaron Copland Collection. Music Division, Library of Congress, Washington, DC.

This is a typescript for "The New 'School' of American Composers." See: "The New 'School' of American Composers."

309. "Zoltán Kodály." n.d. MS. 202/22, Aaron Copland Collection. Music Division, Library of Congress, Washington, DC.

Copland wrote these program notes for the Musical Art Quartet in approximately 1933. After giving a brief synopsis of Zoltán Kodály's career and a comparison to fellow Hungarian composer Béla Bartók, Copland summarizes: "Although his career has been in no way a spectacular one, it has resulted in music of solid worth," especially in chamber music. Kodály's use of Hungarian folk songs for thematic material in his Quartet Op. 2 created "an extraordinary freedom and inventiveness both in rhythm and in melody." To appreciate the modernism of Kodály's Quartet Op. 2, "consider that in 1908 Debussy and Ravel were little known outside of France and Stravinsky was unheard of."

310. "[Zoltán Kodály—80th Birthday]," 1962. MS. 202/23, Aaron Copland Collection. Music Division, Library of Congress, Washington, DC.

This letter commemorating Zoltán Kodály's eightieth birthday was sent to the Hungarian Association of Musicians, to be published in the musicological journal *Magyar Zene*. Of Kodály Copland writes: "He is known throughout America for the straightforward, human qualities of his music:—for its warmth, its humor, its liveliness, its honest and clean 'face.' His folk-lore investigations, along with those of Béla Bartók, are an incentive for younger musicians to follow."

311. "Zurich: 1926."

See: "Playing Safe at Zurich" and "European Festivals and Premieres: A Glance Backward."

2. Copland and Coauthors

312. Copland, Aaron, and Jack Diether. "Guide to Record Collecting; Aaron Copland Suggests a Basic Mahler Library." *Hi-Fi Music at Home,* 4 (March–April 1957): 26, 66–70.

Copland recommends to record collectors a nucleus of five compositions by Gustav Mahler: *Das Lied von der Erde, Kindertotenlieder,* and the Symphonies No. 1, 4, and 9. Jack Diether completed the majority of the article by reviewing current recordings of each composition.

313. Copland, Aaron, and Vivian Perlis. "Looking Back with Aaron Copland." *New York Times Magazine,* 9 September 1984, pp. 82, 96, 98, 100, 104–105.

This article, written with Vivian Perlis, is extracted from *Copland: 1900 through 1942.* The topics covered in the article are Symphony for Organ and Orchestra, *Vitebsk, El Salón México, Billy the Kid,* and *Lincoln Portrait.*

C. Interviews

314. "Aaron Copland Talks about American Music Today." *Times* [London], 20 August 1958, p. 11.

This interview coincided with Copland's appearance in London to conduct his *Orchestral Variations* and "Hoe-Down" in a Promenade Concert. Copland was distressed that each performance of American music in England was treated as "a brand-new import," despite an accumulation of compositions in the United States that comprised an American school of composers. For Copland, there was "no contradiction" between his nationalistic and "cosmopolitan" idioms, since he wrote "as the musical medium suggests." Copland and other American composers were alarmed by the public's "retreat" to recorded rather than live performances of contemporary music.

315. Barnes, Patricia. "Aaron Copland on a Lifetime of Music." *Times* [London], 27 November 1980, p. 11.

On the occasion of his eightieth birthday, Copland reminisced on his musical childhood, his education in France, Nadia Boulanger, his piano music, *Appalachian Spring,* Americanism in music, and the future health of the American musical culture.

316. Bessom, Malcolm E. "Conversation with Copland." *Music Educators Journal,* 59 (March 1973): 40–49.

Malcolm Bessom, editor of the *Music Educators Journal,* conducted this interview with Copland during the composer's three-day residency at West Virginia University. Bessom and Copland discuss topics ranging from American music (its relationship to the contemporary audience, musical Americanism, programming, the Great American Composer, neglected or forgotten composers, and important developments in the 1920s and 1930s), contemporary musical genres (rock, jazz, Third Stream, aleatoric, and electronic music), musical figures (Paul Rosenfeld and Carl Ruggles), Copland's compositional career (his unified compositional approach, desire to write a string quartet, film music, early compositional influences, and position in American musical history), and the qualities of an outstanding music teacher. The article also includes a discography of Copland conducting his own compositions, of Copland as pianist for his own compositions, selected recordings not in the above, and Copland's then unrecorded compositions.

317. Brant, LeRoy V. "America, Involved in Music, Is Becoming Great in Music." *Etude,* 71 (April 1953): 9, 57.

Although the career of the concert artist is "more exacting than ever," there are many more opportunities for professional involvement in music because of the increasing number of musical organizations. Musical talent in the United States has become comparable to that in Europe because of the increased daily involvement in music, "the basis for greatness in music." Copland lists three criteria for an aspiring professional musician: One must have a "compulsion" for music, be friendly, and be accessible.

318. Bredemann, Dan. "Audience Is First—Copland." *Biography News,* 1 (February 1974): 144.

Dan Bredemann and Copland discuss the inordinate emphasis placed on musical masterpieces by conductors, managers, and audiences. Copland applauds the improving situation for composers, in part through the university, but laments that modern music remains unintegrated into general musical life. Copland considers his relationship to an audience and the effect of his writings on opening the minds of the symphonic listeners. The interview, originally printed in the *Cincinnati Enquirer* on 13 January 1974, includes a brief history of Copland in Cincinnati.

319. Burton, Humphrey. "The Art and Life of Aaron Copland." *Listener,* 16 December 1965, pp. 987–990.

This interview was primarily a chronological overview of Copland's career, including topics such as his discovery of Americanism in France, anti-German sentiment, Nadia Boulanger, influence of jazz, Igor Stravinsky, 1930s democratization of music, influence of folk music, the modern symphony, audience accessibility, the "disease" of conducting, and compositional and creative process.

320. Caine, Milton A. "Comments on Copland." *American Record Guide,* 44 (November 1980): 4–6.

Although several other topics are covered (Copland's first musical memory, why he composed no grand opera, his conducting career, and the sophisticated vs. wide audience), Milton Caine constantly returns to the question of Copland's no longer composing.

321. "Classical or Modern: Aaron Copland Questions a Common Musical Distinction." *Times* [London], 28 April 1960, p. 6.

Focusing on the supposed distinction between "classical" and "modern" music, Copland discusses the relationships of nineteenth-century and modern music to contemporary culture, his enthusiams for the music of other composers (François Couperin, Christoph Gluck, Henry Purcell, Domenico Scarlatti, and Igor

Stravinsky), the changing reception of J. S. Bach (and hopefully contemporary composers), the limited taste of concert promoters and their lack of attention to the more adventurous record-buying public, and the phenomenon of George Gershwin.

322. Cone, Edward T. "Conversation with Aaron Copland." *Perspectives of New Music,* 6 (Spring–Summer 1968): 57–72. (Reprint—In *Perspectives on American Composers.* Edited by Benjamin Boretz and Edward T. Cone, pp. 131–146. New York: W. W. Norton, 1971. 268 p. ISBN 393005496. ML 200.1 B67.)

The first half of the interview repeats standard biographical information appearing in "Composer from Brooklyn: An Autobiographical Sketch." In the second half of the interview, Edward Cone, also a composer, and Copland discuss compositional issues: Copland's stylistic periods, his use of the twelve-tone method, differences between Germanic and French composition, implications for university-trained composers, the teaching of composition, and travel and artistic communities (the MacDowell Colony and Tanglewood) to enlarge a composer's "field of vision."

323. "Copland Recalls Criticism." *New York Times,* 3 November 1980, sec. C, p. 20.

Copland recalls playing *Grohg* for Sergey Koussevitzky, in the presence of Sergei Prokofiev, who blurted out at its conclusion, "'Too many bassi ostinati.'"

324. Cox, Ainslee. "Copland on the Podium." *Music Journal,* 29 (February 1971): 27, 50, 55.

Although an interview, the insights of the author on Copland's conducting career are more extensive and specific than Copland's. The author compares Copland to other composer-conductors, connects Copland's conducting career to his lifelong promotion of twentieth-century and American music, and evaluates Copland as a conductor. Copland discusses why his music never caught on with the French, what music he programmed when conducting, the generation of American composers preceding him, and the viability of the modern symphony orchestra.

325. Davis, Dana. "A Copland Portrait." *Instrumentalist,* 33 (March 1979): 25-26.

Dana Davis, a band director in Anaheim, California, interviewed Copland at the California Institute of the Arts in Valencia. The interview focuses on Copland's conducting, covering topics from how and why he began conducting, to Sergey Koussevitzky's influence as conductor, to how other conductors have influenced Copland's conception of his own compositions. Of particular interest is Copland's discussion of the conductor's memorization of scores as limiting to the already characteristically routine concert repertoire.

326. Dickinson, Peter. *First American Music Conference, Keele University, England, April 18-21, 1975.* Keele: University of Keele, 1977. 201 p. ML 200.1 A5 1975.

This interview between Peter Dickinson and Copland appeared in the proceedings of the First American Music Conference, presented by the University of Keele music department and its Centre for American Music and the United States Information Service. Copland discusses topics such as the necessity of his activities beyond composing, the "hindrance" of being a concert composer in the film industry, Copland's passion for conducting, how he selected the poems by Emily Dickinson, and the effects of commission and purpose on his compositional language.

327. Ford, Christopher. "Copland, the Conductor." *Washington Post,* 15 June 1972, sec. B, p. 15.

Although Copland tried to denounce the "tendency to split me down the middle," the author persists, describing two Coplands, both musically and personally. The author focused more on Copland's lack of composition than on his conducting.

328. Freedman, Guy. "A Copland Portrait." *Music Journal,* 35 (January 1977): 6-8.

In this interview Copland discusses the categorization of his works as functional or austere, the finances of composing, his reactions to electronic music, and the contributions and limitations of jazz. He also gives advice for young composers on getting their music played.

329. Freeman, John. W. "The Reluctant Composer: A Dialogue with Aaron Copland." *Opera News*, 27 (26 January 1963): 8–12.

Copland and John Freeman discuss the attraction of composers to opera, "*la forme fatale,*" despite the inherent drawbacks to operatic composition: the enormous investment of time with no guarantee of success, the variable performing forces involved in each staging of the same opera, and the difficulty of gaining practical experience for novice opera composers. For Copland, the primary requisite for a successful opera composer is the ability to "keep a sense of the flow of the action." After a discussion of twentieth-century operas and composers advancing new solutions to old problems (Claude Debussy, Alban Berg, and Kurt Weill), Copland declares that the operatic genre, like individual operas, must have "flow and movement; it has to progress."

330. Frymire, Jack. "Copland 68." *Music & Artists,* 1 (November 1968): 18–19, 48–49.

In this interview, Copland discusses his current conducting career and the differences between conducting British, German, and American orchestras. Although for four decades Copland wrote articles identifying promising young composers, he would not attempt to define the current decade, as the musical scene had become "too complex" with electronics and mass media. Other topics covered include the initial reception of Charles Ives's music, Nadia Boulanger's teaching, Copland's "stylistic guises," *Appalachian Spring,* and his other theatrical compositions.

331. Gagne, Cole, and Tracy Caras. "Aaron Copland." In *Soundpieces: Interviews with American Composers,* pp. 102–113. Metuchen, NJ: Scarecrow Press, 1982. xviii, 418 p. ISBN 0810814749. ML390 .S668.

This interview, conducted in 1975, was originally broadcast over WFUV-FM radio of Fordham University in New York. Perhaps because the interviewers were not musicians, the discussion is less repetitive than many of Copland's interviews. Among the topics discussed are Copland's use of serial techniques, origins of his "accessible" and "abstract" styles, the role of collaboration in the shaping of musical ideas, the effect of titles on the audience, women composers, and electronic, chance, ballet, and film music. The substantial article includes a chronological catalog of Copland's compositions.

332. Gold, Don. "Aaron Copland: The Well-Known American Composer Finds Virtues and Flaws in Jazz." *Down Beat,* 1 May 1958, pp. 16, 39–40.

Copland describes jazz as "a special area of music, with great attractiveness, but with serious limitations." In this interview he discusses what jazz means to him, progressive jazz, commercialization of jazz, the influence of jazz on art music and his compositions specifically, the "plight" of the jazz musician, and specific jazz musicians (Louis Armstrong, Miles Davis, Duke Ellington, Jimmy Giuffre, Stan Kenton, Teo Macero, Shelly Manne, Charlie Mingus, and George Russell).

333. Gräter, Manfred. "Aaron Copland besucht Europa." *Melos,* 24 (April 1957): 108–110.

Topics covered in this interview include Copland's conducting, his recent compositions, film music, his use of the twelve-tone technique, impressions of German musical life, promotion of New Music in the United States, young American (Lukas Foss, Leon Kirchner, and Harold Shapero) and European (Pierre Boulez, Luigi Nono, Karlheinz Stockhausen) composers, and German impressions of American musical culture.

334. Hall, Roger. "Aaron Copland—An Interview with Roger Hall." *Journal of Church Music,* 24 (February 1982): 6–7, 9.

Essentially the same interview as "Aaron Copland's 'Simple Gifts,'" with the inclusion of topics such as why Copland had never written a Mass or cantata, why so few composers could make a living from composing, and why Copland had stopped composing. The article includes a list of Copland's choral and vocal works.

335. ———. "Aaron Copland's 'Simple Gifts.'" *The Sonneck Society for American Music Bulletin,* 16 (Fall 1990): 106–107.

In this interview Roger Hall, a composer and musicologist who has studied Shaker music and dance extensively, questions Copland about his selection of "Simple Gifts" for *Appalachian Spring* and *Old American Songs*. Copland describes his fondness for "Simple Gifts" and the "instinctive feeling of empathy" he would have with a specific tune in a book of folk songs.

336. ———. "An Interview with Aaron Copland." *The Shaker Messenger*, 3 (Summer 1981): 7. (Reprint—In *The Story of 'Simple Gifts': Shaker Simplicity in Song*. 2d ed. Holland, MI: The World of Shaker, 1990. ML3178 .S5H3 1990.)

Essentially the same interview as "Aaron Copland's 'Simple Gifts,'" with the inclusion of topics such as the effect of the orchestral pit in the Library of Congress on the original instrumentation of *Appalachian Spring*, Copland's opinion on a band arrangement of "Simple Gifts," and the Shakers' pleasure with Copland's setting of "Simple Gifts."

337. Hamilton, David. "An Aaron Copland Photo Album." *High Fidelity/Musical America*, 20 (November 1970): 56–63.

The article consists of several pictures in each of the categories: Early Years, Paris, Organizer and Catalyst, Composer for Theater and Films, Teacher, Ambassador, and Conductor. A conversational paragraph—sometimes quoted from "Composer from Brooklyn: An Autobiographical Sketch"—accompanies each picture.

338. Henahan, Donal. "He Made Composing Respectable Here." *New York Times,* 8 November 1970, sec. 2, p. 17.

Much of this interview is Copland's rebuttal to a then recent *High Fidelity* article, in which Leonard Bernstein "chided" Copland for abandoning his simpler style for the twelve-tone method and "painted" Copland as having been forgotten by young composers. Topics Copland discusses range from Virgil Thomson, Charles Ives, and Arnold Schoenberg to the passing need for a distinctive Americanism in music, Copland's lack of compositional influence since World War II, his ambivalence toward electronic music, and his withdrawal from contemporary music and social circles.

339. Hershowitz, Alan. "Aaron Copland: The American Composer Shares His Mind." *Music Journal*, 39 (March–April 1981): 9–12.

Much of this interview focuses on Copland's responses to contemporary new music: current viability of Americanism in music, rhythm in the twentieth century, the symphony orchestra, minimalism, electronic music, and serial music. Copland also reflects on the origins of Western connotations in his Americana, his film music, and his more "serious" works such as *Connotations*.

340. Heylbut, Rose. "America Goes to the Ballet: A Conference with Aaron Copland." *Etude*, 66 (July 1948): 401, 450–451.

This interview is virtually a primer for ballet composition. Copland discusses topics such as the aesthetic battle between ballet and modern dance, the upsurge in interest in dance, his previous ballets, and the economic advantages of ballet commissions. He reminds the potential ballet composer of the balance between score and choreography, the steps of collaboration between composer and choreographer, and the less professional quality of ballet orchestras. While the ballet composer should employ simpler textures and a sharper rhythmic drive, ultimately, the "power and integrity of expressiveness override all matters of aesthetic."

341. Isacoff, Stuart. "Copland at 80: A Birthday Interview." *Keyboard Classics*, 1 (March/April 1981): 5–7.

Copland discusses familiar topics such as his early interests in contemporary music, his musical education in Paris, musical personalities (Nadia Boulanger, Rubin Goldmark, and Elliott Carter), his particular harmonic style, his "decision" to communicate with the wider audience, the role of the piano on his compositional process, and advice for young musicians.

342. Johnson, Harriett. "Aaron Copland: Dean of American Composers." *International Musician*, 75 (July 1976): 6, 17.

Copland talks about the passion that "he willingly has let just about overwhelm him late in life"—conducting. Although Copland gives the impression that he "just 'grew' into conducting" at Tanglewood, he argues nonetheless for a craft of conducting that must be absorbed. Copland describes the feeling of being in front of an orchestra, particularly the Philadelphia Orchestra. As a composer, the joy of conducting your own work is the opportunity to perform the piece as it is heard in your head.

343. Jones, Robert. "Aaron Copland: Musician of the Month." *High Fidelity/Musical America,* 25 (November 1975): MA6–MA7.

With rather standard responses, Copland answers questions about his age, conducting, music critics, serialism, electronic music, and lack of current composing. The interview does contain a fairly substantial discussion of Copland's contributions to a school of American composers. Copland admits that he is "talked out" after having written four books.

344. Karsh, Yousuf. "Aaron Copland." In *Portraits of Greatness,* p. 54. London: Thomas Nelson & Sons, 1959. TR 680 .K3.

While only one page accompanied by a photographic portrait, this interview accurately summarizes Copland's concerns ("the problem of communication between composer and listener") and philosophies ("Art and the life of art must mean something, in the deepest sense, to the everyday citizen").

345. Keener, Andrew. "*Gramophone* Perspective: Aaron Copland." *Gramophone,* 58 (February 1981): 1072, 1076.

This article is primarily an analysis of Copland's career by the author, interspersed with quotations from printed sources. Among the topics covered are a comparison of Copland's childhood discovery of music with his late-in-life discovery of conducting, Copland's apprehension toward the permanence of the printed word, his musical education in France, his "serious" compositions, reminiscences of Samuel Goldwyn, the roots of an American voice in 1920s France, and *Appalachian Spring.*

346. Kenyon, Nicholas. "The Scene Surveyed." *Music and Musicians,* 24 (November 1975): 22–23.

After discussing conducting (his "late passion"), Copland covers topics such as the neglect of his later works, composition in the university, and whether the struggle to create an identifiably American music has been won. While the quantity of composers and their compositions on recordings make it difficult to survey the American scene, David Del Tredici, Charles Wuorinen, and George Crumb are "promising figures." For Copland, no conductor had succeeded Sergey Koussevitzky as a champion of young composers.

347. "A Leading Composer Looks at American Music Today." *U.S. News and World Report*, 81 (4 October 1976): 68.

In this brief interview, Copland reviews the effects of changes during his career. He discusses the loss of an American inferiority complex, the establishment of an American style of music, the perceived naivete of Americans by the French, how cultural exchanges aided the resolution of the cold war, and Thomas Jefferson as a great leader.

348. Mayer, William. "The Composer in the U.S. and Russia: A Frank Talk between Copland and Khachaturian." *ASCAP Today*, 3 (June 1969): 22–25.

The joint interview of Copland and Aram Khachaturian by a third composer, William Mayer, leads to interesting cross-cultural reflections on the differences between genres, audience, and governmental support in the United States and Russia. Copland and Khacharturian compare responses on nationalism in music and compositional process. Copland says that working with a choreographer was easier than working with a film director; Khachaturian had the opposite experience.

349. ——. "Interview with Aaron Copland and Aram Khachaturian." *Composer* (US), 2 (September 1970): 44–47.

This is a slightly abbreviated version of "The Composer in the U.S. and Russia: A Frank Talk between Copland and Khachaturian." The topics covered include a comparison of individual compositional style, audiences, ballet composition, nationalism, and governmental support of composers.

350. Newman, Bill. "Aaron Copland." *Gramophone*, 36 (February 1959): 396.

This interview primarily consists of the author's subjective observations of Copland's personality. In 1959 Copland's favorite conductors of his own compositions were Sergey Koussevitzky, Leonard Bernstein, and Antal Dorati. Bill Newman cites Copland's best known work as *El Salón México*.

351. Nichols, Lewis. "Talk with Aaron Copland." *New York Times,* 19 October 1952, sec. 7, p. 47.

Copland discusses his Charles Eliot Norton lectures at Harvard University, the subsequent book (*Music and Imagination*), and his literary writing. He quickly turns to the issues of programming of contemporary and American music, the hardship of young composers getting their music performed, and the results of university teaching on composers.

352. Orga, Ates. "Aaron Copland Talks to Ates Orga." *Hi-Fi News and Record Review,* 26 (December 1981): 75, 77.

In this interview, Copland discusses composers (Benjamin Britten, Carlos Chávez, Henry Cowell, George Gershwin, Sergei Prokofiev, and Dmitri Shostakovich), his compositional process (use of the piano, revision, and sketches), his championing of contemporary music, his motivations for composing with the serial technique, his lack of recent composition, the changing definition of musical avant-garde, and how to gauge the musical public for a composition.

353. Overton, James L. "It's a Very Lively Scene . . . We're in Good Shape." *San Francisco Chronicle,* 12 March 1978, WOR, p. 49.

In this brief interview Copland discusses his conducting career, his role as spokesperson for American music, other conductors' interpretations of his music, and the proliferation of composers since 1900.

354. Ramey, Phillip. "Copland and the Dance." *Ballet News,* 2 (November 1980): 8–12, 40.

The majority of this interview traces the history, scenarios, and collaborative relationships surrounding Copland's ballets. There are additional sections covering topics such as the influence on Copland of Sergei Diaghilev's Ballets Russes, the Ballets Suédois, and Igor Stravinsky's ballet scores. He discusses several compositional and aesthetic issues relating to ballet scores such as imposed formal structures and choreographers' staging of his concert music.

355. ———. "Copland at 80." *Ovation,* 1 (November 1980): 8–14, 43. (Reprint—*Chicago,* 30 [January 1981]: 122–124, 148–149.)

In one of the more substantial of Copland's interviews commemorating his eightieth birthday, he discusses musical associates (Samuel Barber, Leonard Bernstein, Elliott Carter, Roy Harris, Charles Ives, Sergey Koussevitzky, Walter Piston, William Schuman, Roger Sessions, and Virgil Thomson). Copland reviews the role of the piano compositions in his oeuvre, and the fate of *Piano Variations*, Piano Sonata, and *Piano Fantasy,* specifically. He similarly reviews the reception of his *Symphonic Ode,* Third Symphony, and *Connotations* in comparison to his Americana compositions. Copland also discusses his compositional process.

356. Rorem, Ned. "Where Is Our Music Going?" In *Music and People,* pp. 211–213. New York: G. Braziller, 1968. 250 p. ML60 .R784 M9.

In this brief interview, Ned Rorem poses the question of the future of American music. Instead of a prediction, Copland alludes to the splintering of the current music scene by composers such as John Cage and Milton Babbitt, the university as the site for the avant-garde, an intimidating complexity of much contemporary music, and the passing of the classical symphony. Copland feels that only his scores such as *Connotations* and *Inscape* were an influence on the current generation of young composers.

357. Rosenberg, Deena, and Bernard Rosenberg. "Aaron Copland." In *The Music Makers,* pp. 31–38. New York: Columbia University Press, 1979. xiii, 466 p. ISBN 0231039530. ML 385 .R8.

The first half of this interview gives standard biographical information: Copland's musical education, his conducting and compositional career, his studies with Nadia Boulanger, and the Parisian and American musical scene in the 1920s. Copland then discusses compositional issues such as American musical nationalism, the situation for the contemporary composer (universities, publishers, and support systems), and his own compositional style—how writing for a specific context or performer shaped his output.

358. Rosenwald, Peter J. "Aaron Copland Talks about a Life in Music." *Wall Street Journal,* 14 November 1980, sec. 1, p. 31.

Copland briefly covers the following topics in this interview: his musical education in Paris, the influence of the French school of composers, Martha Graham's commissioning of *Appalachian Spring,* and his entry into conducting.

359. Rothstein, Edward. "Fanfares for Aaron Copland at 80." *New York Times,* 9 November 1980, sec. 2, pp. 21, 24. (Reprint, abridged—"Copland at 80: Still THE American Composer." *San Francisco Chronicle,* 23 November 1980, Review, p. 19. Also Reprint—*New York Times Biographical Service,* 11 [November 1980]: 1526—1528.)

Mostly an analysis of Copland's career and aesthetic by the author, this interview includes a few observations by Copland about his childhood musical education, his studies in Paris, and the relationship of the composer to the audience.

360. Silverman, Robert. "Aaron Copland: Happy Birthday." *Piano Quarterly,* 28 (Fall 1980): 5-6.

In this brief interview, Copland answers questions about why he was no longer composing, his thoughts on the contemporary music scene, and the differences between recorded and live music.

361. "Six on the State of Music." *Music Magazine and Musical Courier,* 163 (October 1961): 23–24.

Copland acts primarily as moderator of the panel (Richard Burgin, associate conductor, Boston Symphony; Arthur Fiedler, conductor, Boston Pops; Erich Leinsdorf, conductor, Metropolitan Opera; Leonard Bernstein, musical director, New York Philharmonic; and Gary Graffman, pianist) in this transcription of the CBS Radio Network program "The Direction of Music in America." The panel discusses the future of the symphony orchestra and symphony musicians.

362. Smit, Leo. "A Conversation with Aaron Copland on His 80th Birthday." *Contemporary Keyboard,* 6 (November 1980): 6–13.

The substantial interview begins with an overview of Copland's career and particularly his piano compositions by Leo Smit, a longtime performer of Copland's piano music. In the interview, Smit balances biographical questions (earliest childhood musical memory, recollections about popular music during his childhood, and working in his father's store) with general questions about Copland's piano experiences (early piano recollections, beginning to improvise, lessons and concerts in Paris), about specific compositions (early juvenilia, vocal compositions, the Piano Concerto, the Symphony for Organ and Orchestra, the film music, *Appalachian Spring*, and Short Symphony), Copland's unique instructional markings in his piano compositions, and reminiscences of Smit and Copland's personal and professional relationship.

363. Soria, Dorle J. "Artist Life." *High Fidelity/Musical America,* 20 (November 1970): MA4-5, 32.

Much of the interview contextualizes Copland's personal life (home, habits, and personality) in the author's voice. Copland discusses his early compositions (and later royalty arrangements with Durand for *The Cat and the Mouse*), his studies in France with Nadia Boulanger, his most successful pieces (in terms of performance and sales), and his current conducting and composing.

364. Stevenson, Joe. "A Conversation with Aaron Copland." *Your Musical Cue Quarterly* (Indiana University), 1 (1973): 21–29.

In a two-hour interview conducted with Joe Stevenson, public affairs program producer for Indiana University's radio station WFIU, Copland discusses such topics as the use of excerpts from his music for television broadcast, his compositional process, stylistic categories ("popular," jazzy/urban, and abstract), music of the 1920s, adoption of the twelve-tone system, recent compositions, contemporary composition in the universities, Arnold Schoenberg in the United States, *Grogh,* Symphony for Organ and Orchestra, Short Symphony, George Gershwin, Benjamin Britten, Copland's support of young composers, aleatoric music, the London Symphony Orchestra, Carlos Chávez, and *El Salón México.*

365. Strauss, Theodore. "What Music Has Charms?" *New York Times,* 23 June 1940, sec. 9, p. 3.

Theodore Strauss's article provides contemporary evidence of how the press still portrayed Copland as the *enfant terrible* of modernism, bravely persevering onward in the face of threats. Copland discusses the role of film music to "do no more than help the film, welding the action and giving it warmth," and the musical conventions already accumulated in the new genre. He also outlines the compositional process for film scores in general, and *Our Town* in particular.

366. Szmolyan, Walter. "Gespräch mit Aaron Copland." *Österreichische Musikzeitschrift*, 22 (October 1967): 612–613.

In this brief interview, Copland discusses his latest compositions, his activities other than composition, avant-garde compositional techniques, and Austrian composers.

367. Taubman, Howard. "Copland's New Opera." *New York Times,* 28 March 1954, sec. 2, p. 7.

In response to why he had not previously written an opera, Copland replies that, until recently, "it wasn't in the air." Copland traces the inception of *The Tender Land* from musical themes, through scenario and librettist. He also discusses the inherent problems of operatic composition: unknown variables of singers, the need for an unobtrusive theatrical flow of all elements, and personal attitudes conveyed through characters.

368. Valencia M., Ernesto. "Aaron Copland, el hombre, el musico, la leyenda." *Heterofonia,* 4 (1972): 9–11.

In this brief interview, Copland discusses his first visit to Mexico, the Salón México, which inspired his composition, compositional responses to the Vietnam War, electronic music, and Latin American composers.

369. Whyte, Bert. "Fanfare for an Uncommon Man." *Audio,* 75 (February 1991): 8–10.

In comments taken from an interview in 1970, Copland discusses his early conducting career, his programming choices as a conductor, his use of serialism, and various recording and playback techniques and preferences.

IV. Secondary Sources— General Studies on Copland's Life and Milieu

A. Biographies and Comprehensive Studies

370. Berger, Arthur. *Aaron Copland*. New York: Oxford University Press, 1953. (Reprint—New York: Da Capo Press, 1987. 120 p. ISBN 0837152054. ML410 .C756 B4. 1987.)

Along with Julia Smith's monograph, Arthur Berger's book constituted the bulk of research on Copland until scholarly interest in the composer reemerged around the American bicentennial. Approximately one-third of Berger's text focuses on Copland's biography, while the remainder focuses on compositional issues. As a composer, Berger took a more theoretical approach than Smith in his discussion of Copland's compositions through the beginning of the 1950s. Berger gives an in-depth analysis of the Third Symphony and supports compositional issues—techniques of chord-building, variations, and declamatory style—with musical examples. Includes three appendices: Musical Works, Recordings, and Chronological List of Copland's Critical Works.

371. Butterworth, Neil. *The Music of Aaron Copland*. New York: Universe Books, 1985. 262 p. ISBN 0876634951. ML410 .C756 B9.

This monograph on Copland's compositions and biography follows Julia Smith's book so closely that it adds little new information on the works that Smith covers. Neil Butterworth discusses the

compositions through 1954, maintaining exactly Smith's categorizations of Americanistic/accessible and abstract/serious. Butterworth's book is most useful in covering works after 1954,
subsequent to Smith's book. The author categorizes these later
works inconsistently by genre (Vocal Music or Instrumental
Music), by compositional technique (Serialism), and by chronology
(Late Works). For most of the compositions, Butterworth gives an
abbreviated history of the composition, the date of premiere, an
anecdote, and a simplified prose description of major themes.

372. Dobrin, Arnold. *Aaron Copland, His Life and Times*. New
    York: Thomas Y. Crowell, 1967. 211 p. ML410 .C756 D6.

This biography was created for young readers and includes a work-
list and bibliography.

373. Pollack, Howard. *Aaron Copland: The Life and Work of an
    Uncommon Man*. New York: Henry Holt, 1999. xi, 690 p.
    ISBN 0805049096. ML410 .C756 P6 1999.

Currently the definitive biography, Howard Pollack's comprehensive and thoroughly researched study of Copland's music and life is
presented in a primarily chronological organization, interspersed
with topical chapters. Unlike Copland's autobiography, written
with Vivian Perlis, Pollack includes insights into how Copland's homosexuality influenced his life and music, as one of many contexts—cultural, historical, biographical, and aesthetic—that
Pollack examined. Pollack stresses the unity of Americanism that
pervades Copland's entire work. He discusses the music in detail,
but without musical examples.

374. Smith, Julia F. *Aaron Copland: His Work and Contribution to
    American Music*. New York: E. P. Dutton, 1955. 336 p.
    ML410 .C756 S5 1953A.

Along with Arthur Berger's book, Julia Smith's work was among
the first comprehensive monographs on Copland's oeuvre and biography. Smith establishes the dichotomies into which Copland's
works frequently continue to be divided: Americanistic/accessible
and abstract/serious. She divides Copland's compositions and musical career through 1954 into three stylistic periods: the first influenced by French composers and jazz (1921–1924), the second

based on abstract techniques (1929–1935), and the third based on American folk song (1934–1955). In retrospect, these categorizations do not address Copland's stylistic unity or allow for the quick succession of styles in his later works. Smith's bibliography is especially useful for Copland's articles written prior to 1955.

B. Significant References to Copland's Milieu

375. DeLapp, Jennifer Lois. "Copland in the Fifties: Music and Ideology in the McCarthy Era." Ph.D. diss., University of Michigan, 1997. 246 p. DA9732066.

In this work, Jennifer DeLapp seeks to explain why Copland, after demonstrating his commitment to the accessibility of style that produced his most popular ballets, turned to the unpopular sounds of serialism in the 1950s. In addition to the aesthetic criteria outlined in his book *Music and Imagination* (1952), DeLapp discusses the political considerations of Copland's choices by examining letters, interviews, newspaper accounts, anti-Communist literature, and government documents. Within this context, she analyzes his *Quartet for Piano and Strings* to show how Copland "created dialogues of other kinds between old aesthetic ideas and new ones, and between musical styles he previously thought incompatible." DeLapp concludes by marveling "at Copland's ability to synthesize seemingly opposing viewpoints and create dynamic new possibilities."

376. Didriksen, Helen. "Aaron Copland's *Twelve Poems of Emily Dickinson*." *Sonneck Society Bulletin*, 17 (Spring 1991): 7–10.

The dedications of each of the songs in Copland's only song cycle have much to say about Copland's musical and social circle, for they are dedicated to twelve composer friends. In 1988 Helen Didriksen communicated with the living dedicatees and other of Copland's friends, as well as Phyllis Curtin, who sang the songs many times with Copland at the piano. In an attempt to understand the connections between the songs and the dedicatees, Didriksen describes Copland's social setting at Tanglewood during the summer of 1949 when he composed these works.

377. Dupree, Mary Herron. "'Jazz,' the Critics, and American Art Music in the 1920s." *American Music,* 4 (Fall 1986): 287–301.

American critics had a wide range of definitions of jazz and an even wider range of opinions on the music. In this study, Mary Dupree explores the three "serious" American composers who combined the jazz and concert idioms—John Alden Carpenter, George Gershwin, and Copland—their works of the 1920s in which they began this synthesis, and the receptions these works received.

378. Friedman, John. "Cat and Mouse." *The Nation,* 18 (December 1995): 775.

John Friedman presents a one-page article on the government's investigation of Copland for "un-American activities." Under the Freedom of Information Act, the FBI released almost two hundred pages of censored documents pertaining to that investigation.

379. Key, Margaret Susan. "'Sweet Melody over Silent Wave': Depression-Era Radio and the American Composer." Ph.D. diss., University of Maryland, College Park, 1995. 513 p. DA9622087.

The purpose of this dissertation is to reconstruct a complete record of network support of new music, to examine the interaction of music, technology, and ideology, and to analyze the music composed for broadcast. After a lengthy introduction covering the history of music and radio, Margaret Key discusses first the cultural context of music on radio, the institutional context, and institutional initiatives. Her discussion of Copland (pp. 181–186) focuses on his *Music for Radio* and presents a brief description of the work, its history, and its reception. Appendix A contains works broadcast between 1929 and 1941 on Network Radio; pp. 312–315 list fourteen works by Copland included in these broadcasts.

380. Lipman, Samuel. "Out of the Ghetto." *Commentary,* 79 (March 1985): 56–62.

The end of Samuel Lipman's article, a discussion of the role of Jewish musicians in classical art music, focuses entirely on Copland. While as a younger man Copland seemed to distance himself from this aspect of his background, he reclaimed his Jewish heritage as he was writing the first volume of his memoirs with Vivian Perlis. Lipman shows that, despite Copland's own claim that "music was the last thing that anyone would have connected with [where I was born]," he benefited greatly from New York's musically rich Yiddish culture in which he was raised.

381. McCall, Sarah B. "The Musical Fallout of Political Activism: Government Investigations of Musicians in the United States, 1930–1960." Ph.D. diss., University of North Texas, 1983. 211 p. DA9401161.

Copland was investigated by the House Committee on Un-American Activities (along with several other composers). Sarah McCall discusses the role that American composers, including Copland, played in various organizations and programs, such as the Composer's Collective and Federal Music Project of the WPA, and describes specific governmental investigations and their effect on individuals and groups. In Chapter 4, she mentions several reports in which Copland and others are listed and discusses governmental investigations of Copland (pp. 62–64). Copland's song "Into the Streets May First" is reproduced (pp. 17–18), and the appendices contain text of reports where musicians, including Copland, are listed by name.

382. Oja, Carol. "The Copland-Sessions Concerts and Their Reception in the Contemporary Press." *Musical Quarterly,* 65 (April 1979): 212–229.

After reconstructing the programs of the Copland-Sessions Concerts (included in an appendix in the back), Carol Oja examines the composers presented in them and the critical response their works received. She concludes, "Despite the censure of their critics, the Copland-Sessions Concerts were a successful undertaking . . . [They] fostered the growth of a new era in American music and promoted a number of young composers at a critical point in their careers."

383. ———. "Cos Cob and the American Composer." *Music Library Association Notes,* 2d ser., 45 (December 1988): 227–252.

Because Copland was intimately involved in the publishing firm Cos Cob, and because much known information about the firm survives only in Copland's letters, the story of Cos Cob is also the story of Copland's early business career. To illustrate the role that the firm played in Copland's career, Carol Oja begins with a brief description of Copland's publishing history before Cos Cob was established in 1929. In her subsequent discussion of the press, she comments on Copland's relationship with Cos Cob, and the press's relationship with other Copland interests, including the Copland-Sessions Concerts and his writings in *Modern Music.*

384. ———. "Gershwin and American Modernists of the 1920s." *Musical Quarterly,* 78 (Winter 1994): 646–668.

After a brief discussion of the origin and ideas of the modernists in the United States, with specific reference to Copland's thoughts, Carol Oja examines the reception of the 1924 premiere of George Gershwin's *Rhapsody in Blue* in the context of the modernists's exploration of jazz-inspired concert music. While elder composers hailed Gershwin's work as a much-needed breath of fresh air, composers of his own generation were threatened by this ostensibly "highbrow" work of a "lowbrow" composer. With the subsequent premieres of Copland's own jazz-inspired works between 1925 and 1927, "Copland was depicted as elevating jazz into art, while Gershwin kept it at the base level of popular entertainment." Oja then focuses on the critical response to Copland's work that consistently elevated him in status above Gershwin and critics' contradictory views toward the fusion of jazz into concert music. Oja concludes with a discussion of the modernists' rejection of Gershwin, in favor of Darius Milhaud, as the model of Copland's jazz-inspired concert music.

385. ———. "The Power of Social Events." In *Cultivating Music in America: Women Patrons and Activists since 1860.* Edited by Ralph P. Locke and Cyrilla Barr, pp. 262–265. Berkeley and Los Angeles: University of California Press, 1997. xi, 357 p. ISBN 0520083954. ML82 .C851 1997.

Carol Oja annotates a guest list that Copland sent to Blanche Walton for an after-concert party in 1930 and discusses how composers like Copland used social events hosted by society women like Walton to build power bases.

386. Olmstead, Andrea. "The Copland-Sessions Letters." *Tempo*, 175 (December 1990): 2–5.

Because both composers saved their letters to at least some degree, there are over one hundred letters comprising almost 450 pages of correspondence between Copland and Roger Sessions. In this brief article, Andrea Olmstead uses these letters to summarize the relationship that blossomed between the composers from 1926 to 1936 and waned thereafter.

387. Parker, Robert L. "Copland and Chávez: Brothers-in-Arms." *American Music*, 5 (Winter 1987): 433–444.

Not only were the educations and early careers of Copland and Carlos Chávez similar, but there were many points during their lives when their professional pursuits met. This essay illustrates several of their shared spheres of activities, including their mutual encouragement and support, the promotion of each other's music, their publishing, teaching, writing, and lecturing; and their ballet, opera, and cinematic compositions. Robert Parker concludes that "the effects of the understanding, sound judgment, and support that accrued to both men out of their long-standing association . . . figure as an inseparable part of the impact each has made on the world of contemporary music."

388. Rosenfeld, Paul. *An Hour with American Music*. Philadelphia: J. B. Lippincott, 1929. 179 p. ML200.5 .R7H7.

From this monograph on American music at the turn of the twentieth century by music critic Paul Rosenfeld, modern scholars can learn how Copland's contemporaries among the musical intellegentsia were judging the young composer before he became a symbol for American music, and before he began his own critical discussions of American and modern music. While Rosenfeld states quite clearly that he did not see any "great composers" in American music, he does consider Copland's music to be "commencing to represent the forces of American life" and to contain "elements of music [that] appear entirely refreshed from the bath of life."

Rosenfeld dedicates ten pages to the analysis of Copland's works prior to 1929, including *Grohg*, his symphony, and his concerto.

C. Articles in Dictionaries, Encyclopedias, Work-Lists, and Catalogs

389. *Aaron Copland: A Complete Catalogue of His Works*. New York: Boosey & Hawkes, 1960. 40 pp. ML134 .C66 A1.

This catalog of Copland's works—divided into a chronological list, classified (genre) list, and alphabetical index of titles—was compiled by his publisher, Boosey & Hawkes. The chronological list is significant since it identifies the publisher, generally Boosey & Hawkes, of Copland's composition.

390. Austin, William W. *New Grove Dictionary of American Music*. Edited by H. Wiley Hitchcock and Stanley Sadie. Vol. 1, pp. 496–504. London: Macmillan, 1986. 4 vols. ISBN 0943818362. ML101 .U6 N48 1986.

This is essentially the same article that William W. Austin wrote for the original *New Grove Dictionary of Music and Musicians*. A few words are different, and it contains one additional photograph. The work-list by Austin and Vivian Perlis contains the same categories as the *New Grove Dictionary of Music and Musicians* list, and the biography is updated through 1985.

391. ———. *New Grove Dictionary of Music and Musicians*. Edited by Stanley Sadie. Vol. 4, pp. 719–725. London: Macmillan, 1980. 20 vols. ISBN 03330231112. ML100 .N48.

This article by William W. Austin, which is essentially the same as the article in the *New Grove Dictionary of American Music*, is the longest, richest, and most detailed of the encyclopedia contributions about Copland. It is divided into three sections—Life, Works, and Style—and contains photographs as well as musical examples. The work-list is organized into these categories: operas, ballets, film scores, orchestral, chamber, keyboard, choral, songs, and writings; the bibliography has forty-eight items.

392. Griffiths, Paul. *New Oxford Companion to Music*. Edited by Denis Arnold. Vol. 1, pp. 485–486. New York: Oxford Uni-

versity Press, 1983. 2 vols. ISBN 0193113163. ML100 .N5 1983.

In this short entry (three paragraphs), Paul Griffiths presents a general discussion of Copland's life as composer, conductor, and teacher; included is a brief survey of Copland's most popular compositions and books. There is no work-list, and the bibliography contains only the biography by Arthur Berger.

393. Jablonski, Edward. *The Encyclopedia of American Music,* pp. 215–217. New York: Doubleday, 1981. 629 p. ISBN 0385080883. ML100 .J28.

A column-long survey of Copland's style and works follows a two-column-long general biography focusing on Copland's early career. There is no work-list, but Edward Jablonski does list Copland's major works within the article; he includes no bibliography. Within the context of the article Jablonski refers the reader to helpful related articles including the League of Composers, the Copland-Sessions Concerts, Cos Cob Press, Marion Bauer, *Music for Theatre,* and Nadia Boulanger.

394. Kennedy, Michael. *Oxford Dictionary of Music.* 2d ed., pp. 192–193. New York: Oxford University Press, 1994. 985 p. ISBN 0198691629. ML100 .K35 1994.

The first paragraph of this article covers Copland's life and career as composer, and the second summarizes his activities as a promoter of American music. The work-list of principle compositions is divided into the following sections: opera, ballet, orchestra, choral, chamber music, piano, and songs. There is no bibliography.

395. *Macmillan Encyclopedia of Music and Musicians.* Edited by Albert E. Wier, p. 376. New York: Macmillan, 1938. 2089 p. ML100 .W64 M3 1938.

This early article on Copland is one long paragraph and contains general biographical material through the mid-1930s, including compositions, books, and other professional activities. The entry contains no work-list or bibliography.

396. Nagel, Rob. *Contemporary Musician.* Edited by Michael La Blanc. Vol. 2, pp. 55–58. Detroit: Gale Research, 1990. 276 p. ISBN 0810322129. ML385 .C615.

This serialized encyclopedia contains a three-page general biography by Rob Nagel written for a nonmusical audience. Basing his work on Arthur Berger, Julia Smith, and the first volume of the Vivian Perlis–assisted autobiography, Nagel covered aspects of style as well as reception, career, and books. The article concludes with lists of selected writings and compositions and a bibliography with seven items.

397. *Norton/Grove Concise Encyclopedia of Music.* Edited by Stanley Sadie. Rev. and enl., p. 184. New York: W. W. Norton, 1994. 909 p. ISBN 033343236. ML100 .N88 1994.

This two-paragraph article presents a general description of life and works. The work-list is divided into the following sections: opera, ballets, film scores, orchestral music, chamber music, piano music, choral music, and songs.

398. Perlis, Vivian. *International Dictionary of Opera.* Edited by C. Steven LaRue. Vol. 1, p. 271. Detroit: St. James, 1993. 2 vols. ISBN 1558620818. ML102 .O6 I6 1993.

Vivian Perlis offers one long paragraph of general biography and three short paragraphs that survey Copland's style and describe his operas. The work-list includes only his operas, but it does give debut information; the bibliography includes books by Copland, interviews, and the major monographs about the composer.

399. Pickering, David. *Cassell Companion to Twentieth-Century Music,* p. 95. London: Cassell, 1997. 409 p. ISBN 0304349372. ML100 .P53 199.

The long paragraph in this dictionary summarizes Copland's life and most popular compositions. It includes quotes by Copland and Leonard Bernstein, but no work-list or bibliography.

400. Ramey, Phillip. *Dictionary of Contemporary Music.* Edited by John Vinton, pp. 148–150. New York: E. P. Dutton, 1974. 834 p. ISBN 0525091254. ML100 .V55.

This dictionary contains a five-paragraph, full-page entry by Phillip Ramey. The first two paragraphs with general biographical information are followed by three paragraphs on Copland's compositional style. The entry includes a list of "principal compositions" and "principal writings." The bibliography lists twelve items.

401. *Random House Encyclopedic Dictionary of Classical Music.* Edited by David Cummings, pp. 135–136. New York: Random House, 1997. 788 p. ISBN 0679458514. ML100 .R29 1997.

This article is two paragraphs long and comprises a general biography with a list of Copland's most popular compositions. The entry includes a photograph and a quote by Copland.

402. Reis, Claire R. *Composers in America,* pp. 77–80. New York: Macmillan, 1938. (Reprint—New York: Da Capo, 1977. 399 p. ISBN 0306708930. ML390 .R38 1977.)

This full page, three-paragraph general biography includes a discussion of Copland's various professional activities. Also included is a work-list dividing Copland's works into orchestral works, pieces for chamber orchestra, choral works, chamber music, stage works, and film music. There is no bibliography.

403. Slonimsky, Nicolas. *Baker's Dictionary of Music.* Edited by Richard Kassel, pp. 195–196. New York: Schirmer Books, 1997. 1171 p. ISBN 0028647912. ML100 .S635.

This article of four long paragraphs covers a general biography that includes information on Copland's compositions, books, awards, and other professional activities. There is no bibliography or work-list.

404. Westrup, J. A., and F. Ll. Harrison. *The New College Encyclopedia of Music.* Edited by Conrad Wilson, p. 140. New York: W. W. Norton, 1976. 608 p. ISBN 0393021912. ML100 .W48 1976.

This entry comprises one long paragraph of general biographical information that includes mentions of Copland's most popular compositions and books. It has no work-list or bibliography.

D. Web Sites

Web sites are sometimes very temporary sources of information—here today, gone tomorrow. The following are the major Web sites as of 20 June 1999 with more than a sentence or two of information on Copland. Where one page has links to others, only the first address is given.

405. http://voodoo.acomp.usf.edu/copland.html

Self-titled The Aaron Copland Homepage, this site links to a biography, an analysis of *Rodeo,* a list of Copland's major works, and a short bibliography of the references used in making this site.

406. http://www.classical.net/music/comp.lst/copland.html

Copyrighted by L. D. Lampson and Classical Net, this seven-paragraph article presents a survey of Copland's style periods, activities, and milieu rather than a strict biography. The discography at the end is organized by title of compositions and lists six of his most popular pieces.

407. http://www.coplandhouse.org

This is the Copland Society home page and leads to sites containing information on the Copland Heritage Association and the Copland Awards.

408. http://www.geocities.com/Vienna/8748/copland.html

Christopher Michaels wrote this eighteen-paragraph general biography that covers Copland's life and career, as well as details on his ballets, especially *Rodeo.*

409. http://www.kennedy-center.org/honors/years/copland.html

This nine-paragraph article presents a general biography, mentioning Copland's most famous pieces and awards.

410. http://www.king.org/today/bios/copland.html

Seattle radio station KING and Naxos recordings have provided this short, three-paragraph general biography that mentions a few of Copland's most popular works. This site also has links to bibliographies and discographies.

411. http://www.mala.bc.ca/~mcneil/copland.htm

This site was put together by Russell McNeil at Malaspina College, British Columbia. While it does not itself have any information on Copland, it serves as a home page to many other Copland-related links, including a biography, library-sponsored bibliographies from the United States and Canada, and commercial pages from publishing and recording houses.

412. http://www.ny.boosey.com/composerpages/copland.html

413. http://www.ny.boosey.com/c2k/c2khome.html

These two sites are maintained by Boosey & Hawkes which continues to publish Copland's music. Although neither of these pages has much information each links to other Boosey & Hawkes pages that offer a wealth of information, including biographies, bibliographies, and commercial sites to help prospective buyers. The second site leads to a large set of annotations by Vivian Perlis on Copland's compositions; these annotations give both specific performance guidelines and short analytical descriptions of the pieces, and are among the few sources on the Internet not available in hard copy elsewhere.

E. Videotapes

The following is a videotape documenting Copland's life, as opposed to videotapes of his works.

414. *Aaron Copland: A Self Portrait.* Directed by Allan Miller; produced and codirected by Ruth Leon; written and coproduced by Vivian Perlis. 60 min. Princeton, NJ: Films for the Humanities, 1986.

Copland, at age eighty-five, looks back on a life synonymous with music in the twentieth century. The videotape features footage of Copland, in addition to interviews with colleagues, critics, and friends such as Agnes de Mille, Martha Graham, Leonard Bernstein, and Michael Tilson Thomas. There is also coverage of biographical context and some performances excerpts such as *Rodeo*.

V. Secondary Sources—Writings about Copland's Compositions

A. Compositional Style

1. Compositional Technique: Form, Harmony, and Melody

415. Cole, Hugo. "Popular Elements in Copland's Music." *Tempo*, 95 (Winter 1970–1971): 4–10.

Hugo Cole discusses how Copland, in the musical climate of the 1920s, in which the dichotomy between the serious and popular composer was growing, retained a unique position as a forward-looking composer who used popular idioms.

416. Creighton, Stephen David. "A Study of Tonality in Selected Works of Aaron Copland." Ph.D. diss., University of British Columbia, 1994. 293 p. ISBN 0315953284.

Stephen Creighton analyzes Copland's use of tonality and tonics in this work to argue that the apparent dichotomy between Copland's "popular" and "serious" styles does not, in fact, exist. He examines tonicizing techniques and pitch classes and presents his results in the form of graphs. He concludes that "these graphs provide useful information about structure in Copland's music because they confirm striking features of Copland's thematic and tonal designs."

417. Dickinson, Peter. "Copland: Early, Late and More Biography." *Musical Times*, 131 (November 1990): 582–585.

Beginning with the premise that "what he composed before going
to Nadia Boulanger shows what he discarded in order to develop
his own impacted conciseness," Peter Dickinson briefly analyzes
several early works including the songs "Old Poem" and "Pastorale," both with musical examples. Focusing primarily on harmony and expressive impact, Dickinson discusses composers who
influenced Copland.

418. Evans, Peter. "Copland on the Serial Road: An Analysis of
     Connotations."

See: Orchestral Music.

419. Kay, Norman. "Aspects of Copland's Development." *Tempo,*
     95 (Winter 1970–1971): 23–29.

With a focus of how Copland's music came to represent an identifiably American style, Norman Kay examines changes in Copland's musical style from the mid-1920s through the 1950s. After
several paragraphs comparing Copland with Charles Ives, Kay analyzes *Music for the Theater* (1925), Piano Variations (1930), and
The Piano Quartet (1950), all with musical examples. Other
works mentioned include the ballets and *Twelve Poems of Emily
Dickinson.*

420. Lynch, John Patrick. "'Emblems': Signifiers of Stylistic Coher-
     ence in the Formulation of an American Sound in This and
     Other Selected Works of Aaron Copland." Ph.D. diss., Uni-
     versity of Cincinnati, 1996. 115 p. DA9734936.

In order to demonstrate that Copland achieved stylistic coherence
throughout his works, John Lynch examines *The Tender Land,
Four Piano Blues, Inscape,* and *Emblems,* and provides a detailed
analysis of the latter work. The traits Lynch asserts to define Copland's sound include Americana themes, jazz elements, harmonic
language and chord voicing, melody, form, and scoring practices.
He concludes that despite *Emblems's* lack of popular acceptance,
the piece "exemplifies Copland's finest work."

421. Mathers, Daniel E. "Closure in the Sextet and Short Symphony
     by Aaron Copland: A Study Using Facsimiles and Printed Edi-

tions." Master's thesis, Florida State University, 1989. 334 p. UMI No. MA1336788. ML410 .C756 M37 1989.

This extensive master's thesis presents an investigation of cadential closure in Copland's *Short Symphony* (1933) and Sextet (1937)—the latter being an arrangement of the former work. Daniel Mathers includes a comparison of manuscript and published sources, as well as a compositional chronology of the symphony.

422. Matthews, David. "Copland and Stravinsky." *Tempo*, 95 (Winter 1970–1971): 10–14.

In this short essay, David Matthews summarizes the influences of Igor Stravinsky on Copland's compositional style in works such as the *Piano Variations* and the *Short Symphony*.

423. McLane, Alexander B. "The Study of African Rhythm as a Model for Understanding Rhythm in Two Representative Twentieth-Century American Works." D.M.A. diss., University of Illinois at Urbana-Champaign, 1992. 173 p. DA9236540.

Alexander McLane proposes an analytical model for rhythm in twentieth-century American compositions based on Western theories of African music and applies this framework in an analysis of Copland's Piano Sonata and Milton Babbitt's String Quartet No. 2. After a lengthy discussion of the creation of the model, McLane analyzes both works together in terms of percussiveness and articulation, interrelationship with other elements of culture, binary/ternary organization, pulse organization, multichronometry, and the relationship between composite, resultant rhythm to individual parts in the music. He concludes that not all categories were equally helpful, but that "the discussions of percussiveness, pulse organization, and multidimensionality were helpful in articulating observations about musical time which might not have found their way into a more conventional analytical method." This work includes sixteen musical examples.

424. Metzer, David. "'Spurned Love': Eroticism and Abstractions in the Early Works of Aaron Copland." *Journal of Musicology*, 15 (Fall 1997): 417–443.

Taking as a starting point a comment made by the composer Samuel Barber that connected sexuality with genres of composition, David Metzer examines eroticism and symbols of homosexuality in Copland's early compositions. He begins by analyzing Eastern and homoerotic references in text and music to four "orientalist" songs: "Spurned Love," "Old Poem," "Pastorale," and "Alone." He also explores the racial and sexual tensions associated with Copland's use of jazz idioms. Works analyzed with musical examples include "Nocturne," "Poet's Song," *Symphonic Ode,* and *Hear Ye! Hear Ye!*

425. Starr, Lawrence, "Copland's Style." *Perspectives of New Music,* 19 (Spring–Summer 1981): 68–89.

In this review of Copland's music, Lawrence Starr states that in the face of such a vastly varied stylistic output, studies of Copland's music must look beyond traditional analytic categories to understand the unifying aspects of his work. After discussing limitations of using such labels as "popular" and "serious" for Copland's music, Starr begins his exploration of compositional techniques common in many works with an analysis of *Piano Variations* and *Music for the Theatre.* He traces structural practices that were common to both of these works that are also found in *Billy the Kid, El Salón México,* and Piano Quartet. Starr concludes that "there exist . . . striking unities among Copland pieces typically seen as representing very different styles and aesthetic attitudes" and hopes that this realization will eventually banish the division in Copland studies "of the useless prejudices that tend to be evoked on all sides when music is labeled 'popular' . . . or 'serious.'"

426. Thomson, Virgil. *American Music since 1910.* Vol. 1 of *Twentieth-Century Composers.* New York: Holt, Rinehart and Winston, 1971. xvi, 204 p. ISBN 030764653. ML200.5 .T45.

Virgil Thomson describes how music in the United States became a mature art in the twentieth century, identifying American musical traits; in his discussion of key figures in this process, he includes a short section on Copland (pp. 49–58). After discussing Copland's activities as a colleague and promoter of new music, he then discusses Copland's music. Thomson credits his own composition as the impetus for some of Copland's stylistic decisions, including the main traits for which Copland has become famous, concluding that "thus it happened that my vocabulary was, in the main, the language Copland adopted and refined for his [works]." Thomson ends his summary by ranking Copland's works within the contemporary American and European musical scenes.

2. Orchestration
To our knowledge, nothing comprehensive has been written on Copland's orchestration—a glaring omission in the study of his work.

3. Americana and Folk Sources

427. Magrini, Tullia. "Aaron Copland: From Practical Music to Unconscious Americanism." *International Society for Music Education,* 10 (1983): 135–140.

After a brief discussion of the stratification of folk, popular, and cultivated musical languages through history, Tullia Magrini examines Copland's American style as resulting not so much from nationalistic tendencies, but from a desire to write practical music that would bridge the gaps between these musics and speak to the American middle class. She then analyzes the folk roots of *El Salón México,* including musical examples of the Mexican folk songs that Copland quoted.

B. Specific Compositions—Instrumental Music

1. Ballets

428. Fuller, Parmer. "Copland and Stravinsky: A Study (Based on the Comparison of the Opening Sections of *Appalachian Spring* and *Apollon musagète*) of the Traditional and Innovative Techniques Used by the Two Composers in Their Search for a Tonally-Based Musical Language in the Twentieth Century." Ph.D. diss., University of California at Los Angeles, 1982. 323 p. DA8225620.

Parmer Fuller analyzes how Copland and Igor Stravinsky approached the task of creating new tonal systems in *Appalachian Spring* and *Apollon musagète*. After discussing each ballet, Fuller juxtaposes the techniques of the two composers, concluding that despite their dissimilar musical personalities, Copland and Stravinsky evolved a new tonal language that was similar in many respects. The second half of the dissertation is a ballet by Fuller, *Twice upon a Time.*

429. Hodgins, Paul. *Relationships between Score and Choreography in Twentieth-Century Dance.* Lewiston, NY: Edwin Mellen, 1992. vi, 227 p. ISBN 077340552X. ML3858 .H6 1992.

With the goal of exploring theoretical, philosophical, and aesthetic connections between dance and music, Paul Hodgins analyzes several twentieth-century ballets including Copland's *Billy the Kid* (pp. 133–164). After a brief summary of the collaboration between Copland and the choreographer Eugene Loring, Hodgins analyzes music and choreography together, illustrating the similar aesthetic approach in each medium. This section contains nine photos of the dance and eight musical examples.

430. Kennicott, Philip. "Dance Music." *Dance Magazine,* 65 (February 1991): 92–94.

In this review of the recording *Music for Martha,* Philip Kennicott describes how conductor Andrew Schenck recorded not just the suite, but the full score of the original chamber version of *Appalachian Spring,* and how he also made other crucial musical decisions such as tempos in different sections, based on Martha Graham's choreography.

431. Knussen, Oliver. "In Search of *Grohg.*" *Tempo,* 189 (June 1994): 6–7.

In this short but informative article Oliver Knussen discusses the composition and reconstruction of *Grohg,* a work that was essentially pillaged to produce Copland's 1929 *Dance Symphony* for an RCA Victor competition. The article also provides a fascinating look into the composer's recycling of material for several other pieces.

432. Lindsey, Roberta Lewise. "An Historical and Musical Study of Aaron Copland's First Orchestral Work: *Grohg,* a Ballet in

One Act." Ph.D. diss., Ohio State University, 1996. 200 p. DA9710609.

With Oliver Knussen's discovery and performance of *Grohg* as a starting point, Roberta Lindsey presents a rich, detailed discussion of this ballet and its place in Copland's work. After introducing her study with a biography of Copland, a history of *Grohg*, and a discussion of its sources, Lindsey analyzes the work focusing on rhythm, melody, harmony, and timbre. She then examines Copland's borrowings of his own compositions by comparing the ballet with later works, including *Cortège Macabre*, *Dance Symphony*, and Scene 8 of *Hear Ye! Hear Ye!* In her conclusions, she challenges the notion of distinct style periods for Copland by pointing out that "there are specific musical characteristics present in *Grohg*, composed in 1922–25/1935, that are also present in Copland's mature compositions. This succinctly illustrates a continuity of musical style."

433. Rober, Russell Todd. "Tonality and Harmonic Motion in Copland's *Appalachian Spring*." Master's thesis, University of North Texas, 1993. 90 p. UMI No. MA1355854.

In this master's thesis, Russell Rober analyzes the tonality and harmonic motion of *Appalachian Spring* in the following categories: "static and dynamic areas, non-traditional harmonies, tonal material used in unique ways, and third-related keys." He concludes that since the work is "not tonal in a traditional sense, is not pandiatonic, is not highly chromatic, and does not employ a double-tonic complex," it is an individualistic example of tonality in the twentieth century.

434. Robertson, Marta. "'A Gift to Be Simple': The Collaboration of Aaron Copland and Martha Graham in the Genesis of *Appalachian Spring*." Ph.D. diss., University of Michigan, 1992. xiii, 376 p. DA9303812.

After tracing the development of musical-choreographic Americanism in Copland's and Martha Graham's compositions, Marta Robertson constructs a "biography" of *Appalachian Spring* based on the correspondence surrounding the commission by Elizabeth Sprague Coolidge and the subsequent collaboration among Copland, Graham, and various administrators. In the second half of the dissertation, Robertson creates a methodology by which the corresponding temporal structures of music and choreography could be compared in a parallel analysis. Through the resultant analysis, based on the shared structures of musical-choreographic time and space, Robertson documents Copland's kinesthetic depiction of Graham's script and her choreographic response to the aural parameters of Copland's score.

435. ———. "Musical and Choreographic Integration in Copland's and Graham's *Appalachian Spring.*" *Musical Quarterly,* 83 (Spring 1999): 6–26.

In this article, Marta Robertson expands on the methodology developed in her dissertation to compare the corresponding temporal structures of music and choreography in Copland's and Martha Graham's *Appalachian Spring.* The components of the methodology—ethnographic work with informant/dancer Peter Sparling and application of the ethnographer's kinesthetic knowledge, in conjunction with the score and videotaped performance of *Appalachian Spring* as "texts"—are explained. With charts showing simultaneous layers of temporal articulations, Copland's and Graham's structurings of formal divisions—movements, sections, periods, phrases, and rhythmic durations—are compared.

436. Shirley, Wayne D. "Ballet for Martha: The Commissioning of *Appalachian Spring.*" *Performing Arts Annual* (1987): 102–123.

Through a plethora of primary sources, mainly letters and photographs, Wayne Shirley explores the less than bucolic origin of Copland's pastoral ballet. "The commissioning of *Appalachian Spring* involved missed deadlines, broken promises, and last-minute substitutions. The principals in the drama of the commissioning must often have felt that they were creating an object-lesson in the folly of government involvement in the arts rather than a work that would serve as a symbol of America." This article does not analyze the music, but rather transcribes many letters pertaining to the commission and collaboration.

437. ———. "Ballets for Martha: The Creation of *Appalachian Spring, Jeux de printemps,* and *Hérodiade.*" *Performing Arts Annual* (1988): 40–73.

Taking as a point of departure a letter from the choreographer Martha Graham to patron Elizabeth Sprague Coolidge, Wayne Shirley reconstructs through a series of letters how a commission for ballets from Copland and Mexican composer Carlos Chávez resulted in ballets from Copland, Paul Hindemith, and Darius Milhaud, and then eventually, Chávez, too. As in Shirley's 1987 article, the content is focused more on the letters of the commission than on the music.

438. Stewart, Louis C. "Music Composed for Martha Graham." D.M.A. diss., Peabody Conservatory, 1991. 325 p. DA9125560. ML3406 .S74 1991a.

Louis Stewart has surveyed the complete body of music written for Martha Graham, tracing the development of her musical-choreographic collaborations from the early days with Louis Horst through her associations with Copland. In the small section devoted to *Appalachian Spring* (pp. 43–58), Stewart's analysis focuses on issues of collaboration and how the music supports the dramatic content. Since this work has no index, the reader is left to find the relevant section from the table of musical examples.

439. Wilkins, Christopher. "Winter Looks at Spring." *Symphony,* 46 (October 1995): 7, 9.

In this short review of a CD-ROM study of *Appalachian Spring,* Christopher Wilkins includes some factual information about the composition and early performances of the work.

2. Film Scores

440. Cochran, Alfred Williams. *"The Red Pony." The Cue Sheet,* 11 (April 1995): 25–35.

In an effort to explain its place alongside *Billy the Kid* and *Rodeo* as works that defined the musical sound of the American West, Alfred Cochran presents a thorough analysis, with musical examples, of Copland's score to *The Red Pony.* He concludes that this work with "such power and sensitivity" is a "masterpiece of film scoring."

441. ———. "Style, Structure, and Tonal Organization in the Early Film Scores of Aaron Copland." Ph.D. diss., Catholic University, 1986. xi, 512 p. DA8627206. ML2100 .C66 S7.

Alfred Cochran analyzes and compares the scores for *The City* (1939), *Of Mice and Men* (1939), and *Our Town* (1940) for their "stylistic characteristics . . . , their method and degree of tonal organization, and specific aspects of their structural unity," concluding that the scores changed "the style of Hollywood film music and [offered] new options to forward-looking cinema composers." Cochran devotes a chapter and appendix to each film. Each chapter briefly introduces the history and narrative of the film in the "Background" section, then proceeds chronologically through the film in a primarily theoretical discussion of musical elements. The traditional formal analysis of the scores does not provide for an in-depth consideration of the integration of music and visual images or narrative. Over two hundred pages of appendices supply musical examples and documentation—correspondence, budgets, musical cue sheets, and outlines—pertaining to each film.

442. Lerner, Neil William. "The Classical Documentary Score in American Films of Persuasion: Contexts and Case Studies, 1936–1945." Ph.D. diss., Duke University, 1997. 307 p. DA9805307.

Neil Lerner examines three films and scores as case studies to explore how the classical documentary film scores provided composers the freedom to write music that surpassed Hollywood's musical limitations. Since Copland wrote scores to both fictional and nonfictional films, his score for *The Cummington Story* (1945) allowed for a comparison of fictional and documentary scoring. After a lengthy analysis of this score (pp. 179–230), Lerner compares it to scores by Virgil Thomson. He concludes that Thomson influenced Copland more than is generally acknowledged, and that Copland's pastoral idiom so famous in such works as *Appalachian Spring* influenced much of Hollywood's musical vocabulary. The analysis sections offer many musical examples, and Appendix 3 contains the narration from *The Cummington Story*.

443. Widgery, Claudia Joan. "The Kinetic and Temporal Interaction of Music and Film: Three Documentaries of 1930's America." Ph.D. diss., University of Maryland, College Park, 1990. 479 p. DA9121449.

This work studies aspects of music and time in film music, using examples that include Copland's score to *The City*. After a lengthy introduction covering theory and traditional analytical approaches for film music, Claudia Widgery introduces new analytical perspectives, including musical gesture, motion as affect, and kinesis. Her discussion of *The City* (pp. 256–315) includes a brief description of the making of the film, and her analysis of the score to *The City* focuses on musical gesture and empathic motion. She concludes that the musical gestures Copland used reflect the rhythms of the images on the screen, "thereby occasioning a viewer's visceral empathy with the experience being depicted." There are ten brief musical examples from the score in the chapter and the text for the narration of the film in an appendix.

3. Orchestral Music

444. Adelson, Robert. "'Too Difficult for Benny Goodman': The Original Version of the Copland *Clarinet Concerto.*" *The Clarinet*, 23 (November–December 1995): 42–45.

In this article, Robert Adelson compares the sketches and early drafts of the *Clarinet Concerto* and examines the changes that Copland made to them for the final version. With the help of letters and other supporting evidence, Adelson identifies the revisions that Copland made at Benny Goodman's request to create an easier version that gave modern performers different options and choices.

445. Evans, Peter. "Copland on the Serial Road: An Analysis of *Connotations.*" In *Perspectives on American Composers.* Edited by Benjamin Boretz and Edward T. Cone, pp. 147–155. New York: W. W. Norton, 1971. x, 268 p. ISBN 393005496. ML200.1 .B67.

After a brief survey of Copland's works that involve even a small amount of serial technique, Peter Evans presents an analysis of *Connotations.* He discusses the structures of the rows used and their treatments in a broad description of the piece through time, showing how Copland balanced the use of the rows both as a strict structural foundation and as the basis for "improvisatory fantasy."

446. Gartrell Yeo, Lisa Lorraine. "Copland's Clarinet Concerto: A Performance Perspective." D.M.A. diss., University of British Columbia, 1996. 121 p. ISBN 0612090833.

In this dissertation, which is directed to the performer, the author discusses the relative influences of jazz styles and neoclassicism. After a description of the historical background and its general stylistic characteristics, Lisa Gartrell Yeo examines the Concerto's structure in detail. This analysis and the subsequent examination of performance practices evident in recordings of the pieces are then applied to specific performance issues of the piece. Gartrell Yeo concludes that the Concerto's reputation as a "lightweight" piece due to its incorporation of popular elements and its connections with Benny Goodman is undeserved, in light of the many traits it shares with French neoclassical works of the 1920s and 1930s.

447. Gippo, Jan. "Piccolo Challenges of Copland's Third Symphony." *Flute Talk,* 15 (October 1995): 38–40.

Copland's Third Symphony offers the piccolo player more prominence as well as more challenges than his other pieces. In this article, Jan Gippo offers advice to piccolo players for achieving accurate intonation in key spots, balance between melodic prominence and ensemble work, and clear articulation.

448. Hess, Carol A. "*El Salón México*: Chávez, Copland, and American Music." *Sonneck Society for American Music Bulletin,* 21 (Summer 1995): 1, 5–8.

After comparing the early careers of Copland and Carlos Chávez, Carol Hess describes the relationship between the two composers that led to Copland's composition of *El Salón México*. The article concludes with an examination of the Mexican themes in both *El Salón México* and Chávez's own *Sinfonia India* and the reception the two works received.

449. Malloch, William. "Copland's Triumph." *Opus,* 4 (February 1988): 22–25.

William Malloch begins his short essay with the story of why Copland cut out eight bars of "keenly important music" from his Third Symphony in the late 1940s. While Malloch primarily reviews two mid-1980s recordings of Copland's Third Symphony, he also reviews the work itself, as well as several live performances of the works he had attended, all to rebut a 1947 *Time* magazine review of the work in which conductor Sergey Koussevitzky was panned as a "lady-kissing 'society' conductor."

450. Matthew-Walker, Robert. "Aaron Copland's Symphonic Legacy." *Musical Opinion*, 114 (February 1991): 48–51.

After debunking what he sees as the myth of Copland's primacy in creating a uniquely American sound, Robert Mathew-Walker surveys Copland's seven symphonic compositions for the composer's largest contribution in music. Matthew-Walker then separately analyzes (without musical examples) the three numbered symphonies, *Dance Symphony, Symphonic Ode, Connotations,* and *Inscape.* He concludes that Copland's populist successes have clouded a true understanding of Copland's real genius as a "great and true original in twentieth-century symphonic writing."

451. Maxey, Larry. "Copland and the Clarinet." *NACWPI Journal,* 35 (Spring 1987): 4–13.

To examine Copland's use of the clarinet, clarinetist Larry Maxey studied seven orchestral pieces. Discussing each piece separately, each with musical examples, Maxey considers the role of the clarinet in the three symphonies, *Billy the Kid, Rodeo, Appalachian Spring,* and the Concerto for Clarinet. He concludes that Copland "demonstrates a keen understanding of the capabilities of the instrument and a willingness to exploit its various strengths."

452. ———. "The Copland Clarinet Concerto." *The Clarinet,* 12 (Summer 1985): 28–32.

In this short article, clarinetist Larry Maxey describes the origins of Copland's Clarinet Concerto with the commission by Benny Goodman, and the reception of the various American and European premieres of the work. Maxey then analyzes both movements of the work, highlighting the role of the clarinet with particular attention to its themes in both movements and the first-movement cadenza. He concludes by stating that, despite a few problems, "clarinetists will forever be grateful to both Copland and Goodman for providing such a marvelous addition to the literature."

453. Steinberg, Michael. *The Symphony: A Listener's Guide*. New York: Oxford University Press, 1995. xvii, 678 p. ISBN 0195061772. MT125 .S79.

Music critic Michael Steinberg collected his program notes written for the Boston Symphony Orchestra and the San Francisco Orchestra for publication by Oxford University Press; all have been revised and rewritten. Pages 128–133 contain his biographical introduction to Copland, in which he briefly discussed Copland's education, commented on aspects of his musical style, and described the style and performance history of his *Short Symphony (No. 2)*.

454. Stier, Charles. "Editions and Misprints: Copland Concerto for Clarinet." *The Clarinet*, 19 (February–March 1992): 48–50.

In this article Charles Stier has compiled a list of misprints appearing in the piano reduction of the Concerto by comparing it with the orchestral score.

455. Whitwell, David. "The Enigma of Copland's *Emblems*." *The Journal of Band Research*, 7 (Spring 1971): 5–9.

Although Copland's *Emblems* for band was long awaited by band directors, it was not well received; David Whitwell surmised that the work "fails to communicate itself" to conductors because of "notational and technical reasons common to much contemporary wind music." In this brief analysis Whitwell attempts to explore and explain these problems to encourage conductors to give the work its due.

4. Chamber Music

456. Barcellona, John. "Performing Aaron Copland's *Duo* for Flute and Piano." *Flute Talk*, 13 (December 1993): 8–11.

Taking Copland's own performance suggestions as his point of origin, flutist John Barcellona presents a careful analysis of the *Duo*, a mainstay of twentieth-century flute and piano repertoire. Barcellona discusses tempo, dynamics, and articulation in both flute and piano parts in order that performers "avoid [a] mediocre performance."

457. Wright, David. "Out of the Attic." *Chamber Music*, 8 (Summer 1991): 9.

Wright has provided a brief (one-page) introduction to Copland's chamber works and their style to encourage performances of this music. His comments on each work easily capture the unique character of the different pieces.

458. Wyton, Richard. "The Copland-Solum Correspondence, 1967–1975: The *Duo* for Flute and Piano Commission." *The Flutist Quarterly*, 17 (Winter 1992): 33–43.

John Solum initiated the commission of a work for flute and piano by Copland, then saved all of the correspondence regarding the commission. In this article Richard Wyton has compiled these letters with a brief commentary.

5. Keyboard Music

459. Adrian, Sabrina Lynn. "Twentieth-Century American Organ Compositions: Selected Composers and Their Works." D.M.A. diss., University of Texas at Austin, 1995. viii, 105 p. DA9617396.

The focus of this dissertation is the development of style within a diverse body of solo organ literature by twentieth-century American composers. After a short introduction to American organ music, Sabrina Adrian examines several works conceived along traditional lines, including Copland's *Preamble (For a Solemn Occasion)*. Her brief discussion (pp. 45–48) begins with a history of the work, includes one musical example, and covers melodic line, phrase structure, harmony, meter, and texture.

460. Anderson, Mark. "Aaron Copland's *Piano Blues No. 3*." *Keyboard Classics and Piano Stylist*, 15 (March–April 1995): 62–63.

In this short article, Mark Anderson presents his own interpretation and analysis as performance suggestions and guidelines for Copland's *Piano Blues No. 3*.

461. Burge, David. "About Pianists." *Clavier*, 26 (February 1987): 46–47.

In the hopes that "many pianists will want to take . . . these pieces into their repertory," David Burge presents a series of articles that surveys several major piano works of the twentieth century. In this article Burge briefly describes Copland's *Piano Fantasy* (1957), in which he believes "Copland sums up his thoughts and feelings about the possibilities of pianistic musical expression."

462. Case, Nelly Maude. "Stylistic Coherency in the Piano Works of Aaron Copland." Ph.D. diss., Boston University, 1984. 2 vols. 1,127 p. DA84116672. MT145 .C6 G370 1984.

In this dissertation Nelly Case addresses the complex, yet consistent, nature of Copland's style throughout his career through detailed study of the four principal works for solo piano: *Piano Variations,* Piano Sonata, *Four Piano Blues,* and *Piano Fantasy.* This very thorough measure-by-measure analysis includes harmonic and rhythmic practice, thematic and motivic procedures, and Copland's approach to serial technique.

463. Lee, Gui Sook. "Aspects of Neoclassicism in the First Movements of Piano Sonatas by Barber, Sessions, Copland and Stravinsky." Ph.D. diss., Ohio State University. 151 p. DA9710513.

In this dissertation Gui Sook Lee compares four works including Copland's Piano Sonata to the classical sonata model in order to illuminate the fusion of the classical form with the twentieth-century idiom. After the introduction which discusses neoclassicism as well as the sonata form, Lee focuses on four themes: proportion of sections, key relationships, parallelisms in the exposition and recapitulation, and the development process, and briefly analyzes each work with respect to these issues. The majority of this dissertation consists of Lee's own composition.

464. McLellan, Joseph. "Airing Copland." *Washington Post,* 21 May 1995, sec. G, p. 12.

Joseph McLellan reviews two recordings of Copland's piano music: *Copland Piano Music—Romantic and Modern* (Cedille CDR 90000 021), performed by Ramon Salvatore, and *Aaron Copland: The Complete Music for Solo Piano* (Sony SM2K 66 345), performed by Leo Smit. While McLellan briefly compares the two recordings, he focuses primarily on an analytical description of the

Piano Sonata in G (included on the first set and not the second), a piece that Copland never allowed performed during his life.

465. "New Music Corner: Aaron Copland." *Keyboard Classics and Piano Stylist,* 4 (March–April 1984): 22–25.

The score to the first of Copland's *Four Piano Blues,* dedicated to pianist Leo Smit, is accompanied by a one-page introduction that briefly surveys Copland's compositional history and piano works, as well as presenting a few of Smit's specific performance suggestions for the first of the *Piano Blues.*

466. Oliver, Michael. "Copland's Other Worlds." *Classic CD,* 32 (January 1993): 44–45.

While Copland's "popular" works are well known, his "serious" works have received a much different reception. In this article, Michael Oliver offers a very brief analysis of the *Piano Variations* in the popular press, attempting to convince the lay audience to give this abstract work a chance.

467. Perlis, Vivian. "Aaron Copland and the Piano." *American Music Teacher,* 40 (October–November 1990): 12–15.

This article is a reprint of an Interlude from *Copland: Since 1943* by Vivian Perlis and Copland.

468. Remson, Michael. "Copland's *Piano Variations:* A Forgotten Masterpiece?" *Piano and Keyboard,* 78 (January–February 1996): 31–35.

Because many pianists find Copland's *Piano Variations* too difficult to learn and to communicate to the audience, Michael Remson offers pianists a means of understanding the compositional intent. Toward this end, Remson presents two levels of analysis of this work: an examination of the theme and the permutations of its motives (with musical examples) and a larger-scale look at the organic cohesion of the work as a whole. The author concludes with performance suggestions to help pianists "communicate the structural and compositional intentions of this work to an audience."

469. Woods, Benjamin. "The North American Piano Sonata in Transition from Tonal to Atonal Styles." D.M.A. diss., University of South Carolina, 1991. 115 p. DA9214983.

This work is a study of ten piano sonatas by American composers for the purpose of illuminating the transformation from tonal to atonal harmonic languages. Benjamin Woods's analysis of Copland's Piano Sonata of 1941 (pp. 29–33) focuses on the link between form and harmony in all movements. Woods's work contains linear form diagrams of all movements and six musical examples from movement one.

470. Worman, Regina Marydent. "The Effects and Roles of Unity and Contrast as Implemented by Composer and Performer of Four Different Periods with Special Emphasis on a Variation Set Representative of Handel, Beethoven, Brahms, and Copland." D.M.A. diss., University of Alabama, 1993. 161 p. DA9403323. ML549 .W67 1993.

In her analysis of four compositions, Regina Worman focuses exclusively on the elements of unity and contrast. Her detailed discussion of Copland's *Piano Variations* (pp. 108–131) presents an examination of these aspects for the theme and each subsequent variation, and includes many musical examples.

471. Young, Douglas. "The Piano Music." *Tempo,* 95 (Winter 1970–1971): 15–22.

After a brief survey of the role of the piano in twentieth-century American composition, Douglas Young presents a summary of Copland's piano works. He analyzes two works, *Piano Variations* and Piano Sonata, in detail with musical examples.

C. Specific Compositions—Vocal Music

1. Operas

472. "Back to *The Tender Land.*" *Ovation,* 8 (August 1987): 6.

This is a brief report on the premiere of the chamber arrangement (for thirteen instruments) of Copland's *The Tender Land.* Believing that the work had been neglected because of its large forces, conductor Murry Sidlin arranged the opera for small ensemble, "with the blessing of Copland."

473. Hillard, Quincy. "*The Tender Land* Revisited." *The Opera Journal,* 20, no. 1 (1987): 27–35.

In a call to "re-assess the opinions . . . [that] placed it in the graveyard of neglected compositions," Hillard Quincy analyzes the plot and the music of *The Tender Land*. He concludes that the work is "a premiere example of American opera."

474. Warrick, Kimberly Johnna. "A Stylistic Analysis of Aaron Copland's Two Operas, *The Second Hurricane* and *The Tender Land*." Ph.D. diss., University of Northern Colorado, 1995. 154 p. DA9617474.

With the hopes that this study will promote further investigation as well as performances of Copland's operas, Kimberly Warrick analyzes and compares the style of *The Second Hurricane* and *The Tender Land*. Warrick devotes two chapters to each work. First, she examines the context, history, plot, and performance requirements, then provides lengthy comments on production considerations and suggestions. Her musical analysis includes motives, growth, jazz elements, rhythm, and harmony; her analytical chapter includes many musical examples. Warrick concludes that because *The Second Hurricane* is dated, a concert performance of some of the choral music would be best; because *The Tender Land* is timeless and the music beautiful, despite some inherent weaknesses, it "deserves a place among the most important twentieth-century American operas."

2. Choral

To our knowledge, there have been no exhaustive studies of Copland's choral work, clearly an area for future exploration.

3. Songs

475. Cherlin, Michael. "Thoughts on Poetry and Music, on Rhythms in Emily Dickinson's 'The World Feels Dusty' and Aaron Copland's Setting of It." *Integral,* 5 (1991): 55–75.

Interpretation of poems can vary widely depending on the edition that is read and the pauses and accents used in reading; a musical setting supports one interpretation by setting the rhythms of its words and pauses. After comparing the punctuation found in the modern standard edition of this poem with the very different punctuation found in the 1929 edition that Copland used for his setting, and after discussing the different meanings of each, Michael Cherlin presents a detailed analysis of Copland's setting of the poem's rhythms and pauses and its subsequent interpretation.

476. Coroniti, Joseph. *Poetry as Text in Twentieth-Century Vocal Music: From Stravinsky to Reich.* No. 35 of *Studies in the History and Interpretation of Music.* Lewiston, NY: Edwin Mellen, 1992. ix, 101 p. ISBN 0773497749. ML3849 .C74 1992.

Joseph Coroniti examines the relationship between text and music in two of Copland's Emily Dickinson settings: "Sleep Is Supposed to Be" (pp. 67–68) and "I Felt a Funeral, in My Brain" (pp. 70–71). Without an index, the reader is left to find these sections from the list of illustrations. Coroniti includes his own personal interpretation in the analysis of text and expression.

477. Friedberg, Ruth C. *American Art Song and American Poetry.* Vol. 1, *America Comes of Age.* Metuchen, NJ: Scarecrow Press, 1981. 152 p. ISBN 0810814609. ML2811 .F75.

In the section on Copland (pp. 117–140), Ruth Friedberg creates a programmatic close reading of the *Twelve Poems of Emily Dickinson,* by correlating text with musical examples from the score.

478. Mabry, Sharon Cody. "*Twelve Poems of Emily Dickinson* by Aaron Copland: A Stylistic Analysis." D.M.A. diss., George Peabody College for Teachers, 1977. 228 p. DA7725117. MT115 .C67 M23 1977a.

Sharon Mabry's dissertation is in two parts; the first part (160 pp.) is on the songs and the second on Schoenberg's *Pierrot lunaire.* Her introduction contains a brief analysis of the poetry, a biography of Emily Dickinson, and a description of the poetic structure of the cycle. Chapter 2, "General Stylistic Characteristics," begins with a discussion of the mood and setting and continues with sections on the accompaniment, vocal requirements, melodic lines, and tonality. Chapter 3 presents a thorough analysis of each song separately and includes many musical examples, discussing specifically the same elements covered generally in the preceding chapter. The section on Copland ends with a short bibliography of seventeen items.

479. Soll, Beverly, and Ann Dorr. "Cyclical Implications in Aaron Copland's *Twelve Poems of Emily Dickinson.*" *College Music Symposium,* 32 (1992): 99–128.

While other studies of Copland's only song cycle find no cyclical construction or overall thematic unities, Beverly Soll and Ann Dorr believe that "intricate musical and textual materials combine to create a highly organized and unique overall structure." After a thorough examination of the texts, the relationships between the texts, and the structure within the order of the texts, they present a detailed analysis of the compositional techniques used in the cycle. This discussion includes spatial effects in the piano accompaniment, syllabification and word repetition, melodic contour, and the use of "color intervals," ostinato figures, arrhythmic figures, and text painting (all with musical examples). Soll and Dorr conclude that while "one is not overwhelmed with a feeling of sameness from song to song . . . it is the small interrelationships . . . intricately woven into the fabric of the cycle which create the comfortable sense of cohesiveness."

480. Young, Douglas. "Copland's Dickinson Songs." *Tempo,* 103 (December 1972): 33–37.

In an attempt to establish its "rightful place in the repertoire," Douglas Young presents a brief analysis of Copland's only song cycle. After discussing melodic contour and syllabification, harmonic language, and texture (all with musical examples), Young examines interpretive meanings of the texts.

VI. Topical Studies

A. Copland as Americanist

481. Kennicott, Philip. "Aaron Copland: Mythical Americana." *Dance Magazine,* 64 (November 1990): 64–65.

In this brief essay, Philip Kennicott discusses the heated criticisms that Copland received for his Americana style and tries to explain the critics' views by comparing American nationalism with the German nationalism of World War II.

482. Murchison, Gayle Minetta. "Nationalism in William Grant Still and Aaron Copland between the Wars: Style and Ideology." Ph.D. diss., Yale University. 634 p. DA9835253.

In this set of case studies, Gayle Murchison compares the development of ideas of nationalism and the "ideal style of modern American music" of Copland and William Grant Still. After an introduction in which this pairing is explained and justified with a comparison of their lives and careers, Murchison discusses both the aesthetics and the styles of Still's and Copland's "New American Music." In the six chapters that focus primarily on Copland, she discusses his relationship with French neoclassicism, jazz, his use of English-American folk songs, Copland's ideas about radio and film, and Still's and Copland's writings about themselves and each other.

483. Sitton, Michael. "Americanism in Music." *Music Clubs Magazine,* 70 (Summer 1991): 30–31.

In this assessment of how American music has come to dominate the Western classical art music scene, Michael Sitton evaluates the roles that Copland and Leonard Bernstein played in the rise of an American style.

484. Starr, Larry. "Ives, Gershwin, and Copland: Reflections on the Strange History of American Art Music." *American Music,* 12 (Summer 1994): 167–187.

In response to typical studies of American styles in art and literature in which differences and eccentricities are valued, Larry Starr searches for commonalities in the music of three quintessential American composers—Charles Ives, George Gershwin, and Copland—to establish "a sense of common enterprise and purpose among American artists and American scholars." He finds that commonality in the way each composer handled the heterogeneity of the American musical experience characteristic of vernacular music, and how each embraced musical diversity. After comparing Ives's musical juxtapositions and Gershwin's musical synthesis, and the unfavorable critical responses both received, Starr turns to Copland, analyzing and comparing his *Piano Variations* and *Appalachian Spring.* He concludes that, as we study American composers, we should not ask why their music exhibits such a wide variety of styles within and between oeuvre, but given the wealth of American musical experiences, "How could an American composer be expected to write otherwise?"

485. Zuck, Barbara A. "Americanism and American Art Music, 1929–1945." Ph.D. diss., University of Michigan, 1978. 615 p. DA7813603. (Reprint—*A History of Musical Americanism.* Ann Arbor, MI: UMI Research Press, 1980. xi, 383 p. ISBN 0835711099. ML200 .Z8.)

Presenting a history of musical Americanism, Barbara Zuck describes the movement in American art music stemming from both social and aesthetic causes that produced a self-defined label of Americanism. After a thorough survey of Americanism through the 1920s by way of an introduction, then a focused study of Americanism in the 1930s, Zuck examines specific composers and specific compositions, including Copland and his *Appalachian Spring* (pp. 473–530). Zuck's discussion of Copland includes a brief biographical sketch, a rich analysis of Nadia Boulanger's impact on Copland and the development of Americanist ideology in music and an American style, Copland's Americanist role, and the American stylistic elements of *Appalachian Spring*. An extensive index provides easy access to references to Copland outside this main section.

B. Copland as Conductor

486. King, John S. "Perlis on Copland: An Interview." *Journal of the Conductors' Guild,* 11 (Summer-Fall 1990): 96–102.

John King's article is a transcription of an interview between King and Vivian Perlis, broadcast on National Public Radio (2 February 1990). It contains anecdotes, presumably from Perlis's books, about Copland and *Appalachian Spring*. Also included is information about Copland as a conductor and specific challenges *Appalachian Spring* presents conductors. The article concludes with a short discussion, unrelated to the ballet, of Copland as a serial composer.

C. Copland as Critic/Commentator/Author

487. Cochran, Alfred W. "The Spear of Cephalus: Observations on Film Music Analysis." *Indiana Theory Review,* 11 (Spring-Fall 1990): 65–80.

Using Copland's writings as his point of departure, Alfred Cochran explains and defends the study of film scores as a legitimate part of the study of the history and theory of music.

488. Lindsey, Roberta Lewise. "A Thematic Annotated Bibliography of the Literary Works and Interviews of Aaron Copland from 1924–1964." Master's thesis, Butler University, 1986. 113 p. UMI No. MA1334260.

Roberta Lindsey has compiled, categorized, and annotated Copland's writings and interviews from 1924 to 1964, evaluating his steady and constant development and growth. She divides Copland's articles into categories: Critics and Criticism (Copland as

Critic and Copland on Critics), Music (Film Music, Private Thoughts, Theory, and Modern Music), and Musicians (Composers, Performers, and Teachers). In addition to evaluations following each section, Lindsey concludes that Copland's literary examinations of issues often preceded his compositional applications. The work includes an extensive People and Compositions index.

489. Meckna, Michael. "Copland, Sessions, and *Modern Music: The Rise of the Composer-Critic in America." American Music*, 3 (Winter 1985): 198–204.

In this brief summary of his 1984 dissertation, Michael Meckna compares the critical writings of Copland with those of Roger Sessions found in *Modern Music* between 1924 and 1934, and assesses their impact on this period of American music. Meckna concludes, "The two complemented and balanced one another and acted as a magnet to a host of [other] composers . . . The results were an invaluable record of music history written by the artists who were making it."

490. ———. "The Rise of the American Composer-Critic: Aaron Copland, Roger Sessions, Virgil Thomson, and Elliott Carter in the Periodical *Modern Music,* 1924–1946." Ph.D. diss., University of California, Santa Barbara, 1984. 273 p. DA8428624. ML200.5 M37 1984a.

Michael Meckna presents a study and assessment of the criticism of the American composer-critic in the periodical *Modern Music*. Organized around critical category (i.e., craftsmanship, vitality, originality, style, and aesthetics) rather than individuals, the four principle composer-critics of the work are discussed continually and equally throughout. Meckna includes criticisms by Roger Sessions, Virgil Thomson, and Elliott Carter of Copland's works, as well as an analysis of Copland's own criticism. A comprehensive bibliography lists thirty-eight articles Copland wrote for *Modern Music*.

491. Reichling, Mary J. "Dewey, Imagination, and Music: A Fugue on Three Subjects." *Journal of Aesthetic Education,* 25 (Fall 1991): 61–78.

In her exploration of John Dewey's *Art as Experience* (1980), Mary Reichling examines his philosophies "in counterpoint with the writings of composers . . . to illustrate and confirm Dewey's theor[ies]." Reichling draws extensively from the writings of Copland, in addition to several others, as countersubjects, to help make Dewey's philosophies relevant to musicians and music educators.

D. Copland as Mentor/Teacher

We could find no exhaustive texts written about Copland's role as a mentor.

VII. Tributes and Obituaries

492. "Aaron Copland." *American Organist,* 25 (March 1991): 25.

493. "Aaron Copland." *Clavier,* 30 (January 1991): 48.

494. "Aaron Copland." *Instrumentalist,* 45 (January 1991): 55.

495. "Aaron Copland." *Nuova Rivista Musicale Italiana,* 25 (April–June 1991): 341.

496. "Aaron Copland." *Das Orchester,* 39 (February 1991): 196.

497. "Aaron Copland." *Variety,* 10 December 1990, p. 101.

498. "Aaron Copland." *Wall Street Journal,* 3 December 1990, sec. A, p. 1.

499. "Aaron Copland." *Washington Post,* 4 December 1990, sec. A, p. 16.

500. "Aaron Copland's Legacy to Support New Music." *Fontes Artis Musicae,* 40 (1993): 276–277.

501. Barnes, Bart. "Eminent American Composer Aaron Copland Dies at 90." *Washington Post,* 3 December 1990, sec. A, p. 1.

502. Berger, Arthur. "Aaron Copland: 1900–1990." *Perspectives of New Music,* 30 (1992): 296–298.

503. ———. "From Copland, the Gift of Complexity." *New York Times,* 9 December 1990, sec. 2, p. 1.

504. Bernstein, Leonard. "Aaron Copland: An Intimate Portrait." *High Fidelity,* 20 (November 1970): 53–55.

505. "A Birthday Scrapbook for Aaron Copland." *Tempo,* 135 (December 1980): 28. (photos only)

506. Cai, Liang-yu. "A Letter from China: In Memory of Aaron Copland." *Sonus: A Journal of Investigations into Global Musical Possibilities,* 12 (Spring 1992): 48–52.

507. "Copland Remembered; Aaron Copland: 1900–1990—Six American Composers Pay Tribute to the Master." *Opera News,* 2 February 1991, p. 33.

508. Dower, Catherine. "Aaron Copland: Giant on the Contemporary Music Scene." *Musart,* 23 (November–December 1970): 10–11, 24–45.

509. "Foundation Commissions in Honor of Aaron Copland." *ASCAP in Action* (Fall 1985): 53.

510. Glass, Philip. "Growing Bold in the Presence of a 'Great Man.'" *New York Times,* 9 December 1990, sec. 2, p. 6.

511. Goodwin, Noël. "Aaron Copland (1900–1990)." *Opera* [London], 42 (February 1991): 167–168.

512. Gould, Morton. "In Memoriam." *ASCAP in Action* (Spring 1991): 31.

513. Greco, Stephen. "Aaron Copland Celebrates [80th] Birthday." *Dance Magazine,* 54 (November 1980): 9–10.

514. Henahan, Donal. "As Kindred As Opposites Could Be." *New York Times,* 16 December 1990, sec. 2, p. 35.

515. Hiemenz, Jack. "Aaron Copland at 85: The Birthday Tributes." *High Fidelity/Musical America,* 36 (April 1986): 2, 11, 40.

516. Hitchcock, H. Wiley. "Aaron Copland (1900–1990)." *Newsletter—Institute for Studies in American Music,* 20 (November 1990): 14.

517. ———. "Aaron Copland and American Music." *Perspectives of New Music,* 19 (Fall–Winter 1980): 31–33.

518. Horowitz, Is. "Noted Composer Aaron Copland Dead at Age 90." *Billboard,* 15 December 1990, p. 8.

519. Kerner, Leighton. "Aaron Copland (1900–90): The Honest Place." *The Village Voice,* 18 December 1990, pp. 69, 98.

520. ———. "Descants: Slender Spikes, Striding Chords (85th Birthday Concerts)." *The Village Voice,* 3 December 1985, p. 96.

521. Kriegsman, Alan M. "Aaron Copland: If America Ever Had a Composer Laureate . . . " *Washington Post,* 8 April 1973, sec. L, pp. 1–3.

522. McLellan, Joseph. "Aaron Copland, American Classic." *Washington Post,* 3 December 1990, sec. C, p. 1.

523. Meister, Barbara. "Aaron Copland: A Recollection and Tribute." *Music Magazine,* 14 (February/March 1991): 8–12.

524. Mellers, Wilfrid. "Aaron Copland: 1900–1990." *Musical Times,* 132 (March 1991): 131.

525. ———. "Homage to Aaron Copland." *Tempo,* 95 (Winter 1970–1971): 2–4.

526. Moor, Paul. "Aaron Copland, 1900–1990." *Musical America,* 111 (February 1991): 14.

527. Perlis, Vivian. "A Farewell to Aaron Copland and Leonard Bernstein." *Sonneck Society Bulletin,* 17 (Spring 1991): 3.

528. Ramey, Phillip. "Aaron Copland, Genial Patriarch of American Music." *Ovation,* 6 (November 1985): 10–14.

529. Rockwell, John. "Copland, the Dean of U.S. Music, Dies at 90." *New York Times,* 3 December 1990, sec. A, p. 1.

530. ———. "Why Aaron Copland and American Music Are Synonymous." *New York Times,* 4 December 1990, sec. C, p. 15.

531. Rorem, Ned. "Copland's Birthday." In *Pure Contraption: A Composer's Essays,* pp. 88–93. New York: Holt, Rinehart and Winston, 1974. vii, 149 p. ISBN 0030110211. ML60 .R784 P9.

532. Salzman, Eric. "Aaron Copland: The American Composer Is Eighty." *Stereo Review,* 46 (February 1981): 66–69.

533. Schuman, William. "More Comments on Copland." *American Record Guide,* 44 (November 1980): 6–8.

534. Smit, Leo. "Aaron Copland, 1900–1990." *Keyboard,* 17 (March 1991): 31.

535. Teachout, Terry. "Fanfare for Aaron Copland." *Commentary,* 103 (January 1997): 56–61.

536. "Uncommon American." *Los Angeles Times,* 4 December 1990, sec. B, p. 6.

537. Von Rhein, John. "Copland: Nearing 80, Still as Fresh as His Music." *Chicago Tribune,* 9 November 1980, sec. 6, p. 7.

538. Weirich, Robert. "The View from the Second Floor." *Clavier,* 29 (November 1990): 46.

539. ———. "The View from the Second Floor." *Clavier,* 30 (February 1991): 46.

VIII. Foreign Language Sources

Few comprehensive foreign language sources focused solely on Copland have appeared since the mid-1980s. In most, Copland is only ancillary.

540. Lively, David. "La recherche du style à travers les oeuvres pianistiques d'Aaron Copland: De la forme consciente à la forme symbolique" ["The Investigation of Style through the Piano Works of Aaron Copland: From Conscious Form to Symbolic Form"]. *Analyse musicale,* 17 (October 1989): 23–30. ISSN: 0295-3722.

RILM ABSTRACT (citation unverified): Copland's three major piano works—the Variations (1930) Sonata (1939–1941), and *Piano Fantasy* (1955–1957)—share a structural property that may be called symbolic form. Analytic discussion of the works leads to speculation on the origin of conscious formal construction and the definition of style.

IX. Bibliographies and Discographies

541. Clark, Sedgwick. "Copland on CD." *Musical America,* 111 (March 1991): 14.

542. Dickinson, Peter. "The Gramophone Collection: Aaron Copland." *Gramophone,* 68 (November 1990): 963–965.

543. Gleason, Harold, and Warren Becker. "Aaron Copland." In *20th-Century American Composers, Music Literature Outlines.* 4th ser. 2d ed., 33–57. Bloomington, IN: Frangipani Press, 1980. ix, 232 p. ISBN 0899172660. ML106 .U3G55 1980.

544. Hamilton, David. "Aaron Copland: A Discography of the Composer's Performances." *Perspectives of New Music,* 19 (Fall–Winter 1970): 149–154.

545. ———. "The Recordings of Copland's Music." *High Fidelity,* 20 (November 1970): 64–66, 70–72, 116.

546. Oja, Carol. "Aaron Copland." In *American Music Recordings,* 62–72. New York: Institute for Studies in American Music, 1982. xxi, 368 p. ISBN 0914678191. Z6814 .P5 A52.

547. "Overview: American Composers." *American Record Guide,* 58 (July–August 1995): 60–64.

548. Skowronski, Joann. *Aaron Copland: A Bio-Bibliography.* Westport, CT: Greenwood, 1985. x, 273 p. ISBN 0313240914. Z6817 .C78S62 1985. (Discography: pp. 29–69.)

Although Web sites change frequently, as do recordings, which regularly go in and out of print, commercial Web sites selling classical music maintain an extensive and current listing of Copland's recordings. We recommend the following Web sites (as of July 1999):

549. http://www.cdnow.com

550. http://www.amazon.com

551. http://www.borders.com

Author Index

Numbers are entry numbers.

Title Index

Numbers are entry numbers.

Subject Index

Numbers are entry numbers.

About the Authors

Marta Robertson specializes in the intersection between music and movement, particularly in twentieth-century American and Latin American musics with dance. Her dissertation (University of Michigan, 1992), "'The Gift to Be Simple': The Collaboration of Aaron Copland and Martha Graham in the Genesis of Appalachian Spring," explored the collaborative artistic process in theatrical dance and introduced a methodology by which a musical score and choreography can be simultaneously analyzed. Currently an assistant professor of musicology/ethnomusicology at Gettysburg College (Gettysburg, Pennsylvania), Robertson is involved in the centenary celebrations of Copland's birth. Her article, "Musical and Choreographic Integration in Copland's and Graham's *Appalachian Spring*: The Revivalist's Solo as Danced by Peter Sparling," appears in the Spring 1999 volume of *Musical Quarterly*. Robertson recently spent a summer in Guatemala and Mexico, where she participated in a National Endowment for the Humanities Summer Institute "The Maya World."

Robin Armstrong teaches music history and literature at Western Maryland College. Her original specialty of Renaissance music has expanded since earning her degree at the University of Michigan to include broad swatches of American music. Also interested in curriculum and pedagogy, she currently focuses on making accessible to students any and every musical topic of interest.

Composer Resource Manuals
Guy A. Marco, *General Editor*

34. ALLESANDRO AND DOMENICO
    SCARLATTI (1993)
    by Carole F. Vidali

35. HENRICUS ISAAC (1991)
    by Martin Picker

36. GUILLAUME DE MACHAUT
    (1995)
    by Lawrence Earp

37. EDWARD ELGAR (1993)
    by Christopher Kent

38. ALBAN BERG (1996)
    by Bryan R. Simms

39. BENJAMIN BRITTEN (1996)
    by Peter J. Hodgson

40. BÉLA BARTÓK (1997)
    Second Edition
    by Elliott Antokoletz

41. JEAN SIBELIUS (1998)
    by Glenda D. Goss

42. GIUSEPPE VERDI (1998)
    by Gregory Harwood

43. TOMÁS LUIS DE VICTORIA
    (1998)
    by Eugene Casjen Cramer

44. ZOLTÁN KODÁLY (1998)
    by Mícheál Houlahan
    and Philip Tacka

45. ISAAC ALBÉNIZ (1998)
    by Walter A. Clark

46. CARLOS CHÁVEZ (1998)
    by Robert Parker

47. SCOTT JOPLIN (1998)
    by Nancy R. Ping-Robbins

48. GIACOMO PUCCINI (1999)
    by Linda B. Fairtile

49. GABRIEL FAURÉ (1999)
    by Edward R. Phillips

50. FRÉDÉRIC CHOPIN
    (1999)
    by William Smialek

51. GAETANO DONIZETTI
    (2000)
    by James P. Cassaro

52. ELLIOTT CARTER (2000)
    by John Link

53. AARON COPLAND (2001)
    by Marta Robertson
    and Robin Armstrong